ORIENTAL
FLAVOURS

ORIENTAL FLAVOURS

An English Cook Travels Eastward

FRANCES BISSELL

PAVILION

First published in Great Britain in 1990 by
PAVILION BOOKS LIMITED
196 Shaftesbury Avenue, London WC2H 8JL

Text copyright © Frances Bissell 1990
Recipe photographs © Graham Miller 1990
Ingredient photographs © Mike Dunning 1990

Designed by MATHEWSON BULL

A CIP catalogue record for this book is
available from the British Library

ISBN 1 85145 277 X

10 9 8 7 6 5 4 3 2 1

Printed and bound in Italy by Graphicon s.r.l.

CONTENTS

ACKNOWLEDGEMENTS

This list contains no order of preference or importance. And, unfortunately, I know it does not contain the names of every single person, whether chef, cook, information officer, public relations officer, food and beverage manager, driver, restaurant manager, airline official, hotel executive, restaurateur, who has helped me in some way in the course of the several years it has taken to write this book. But first of all I thank Tom for sharing my travels with me.

Neil and Bettina Maloney
Chris Kershaw, *Hong Kong*
Jürg Münch, *Hong Kong*
Christian Pirodon, *Hong Kong*
James and Julia Smith, *Hong Kong*
George Strachan, *Hong Kong*
Marjorie Brodie, *Hong Kong*
Jürg Tüscher, *Hong Kong*
Gerrie Pitt, *Hong Kong*
Chan Fat Chee and the Fung
Lum restaurant, *Shatin*
Lillian Chang and
The Peninsula Group, *Hong Kong*
Lyn Grebstad and
The Regent Group, *Hong Kong*
Stanley Hwang and Wen Shan
Yu, *Taipei Hilton*
Heinz Schwander and colleagues,
Shanghai Hilton
Peter Knipp
Robert Riley,
the Mandarin Oriental Group
and their hotels in *Hong Kong,*
Singapore, Manila and *Macau*
Urs Wütrich
Urs Bessmer
Violet Oon, *Singapore*
Julie Lim, *Singapore*
Le Meridien, *Singapore*
The Carlton, *Singapore*
Jackie Ternisien, Christian
Turquier and Janis Beber,
Regent, Singapore

Izan Yusuff and Philippe
Charreaudau, *Regent,*
Kuala Lumpur
Annabel Zimmermann and Peter
Graeme, *Hong Kong*
Cathay Pacific Airlines
British Airways
Hong Kong Tourist Association
Elizabeth Soo,
Kuala Lumpur Hilton
Doreen Fernandez, *Ateneo*
University, Manila
Kevin Sinclair,
South China Morning Post
Karen Cox,
The Regent Group
Robert Hartley
Simon Hirst
Brian Williams, *Hong Kong*
Gillian Stevens, *Hong Kong*
David Bell,
Cathay Pacific, Hong Kong
Peter and Tessa Finamore,
Manila
Millie Reyes,
Manila
Neil Harris,
British Airways, Manila
Carmel and Vera Chow,
Hong Kong and Sydney
and Tricia Hilder as always.

NTRODUCTION

This is not a Chinese cookery book. It is, if anything, an English cookery book, since I am an English cook, cooking in England with ingredients that are available to me locally. But in order to understand and assimilate oriental cooking techniques, ingredients and flavours into my own kitchen, I felt I had to learn as much as possible about how they were used in their natural environment, and this has led my husband, Tom, and I to travel extensively in the Far East over the last five years.

Some of my friends and colleagues in the cookery world abhor the thought of bastardized cuisines and feel that they will eventually lead to the decline of authentic recipes and culinary traditions. I think that their fear is unfounded, simply because there are so many cooks and culinary historians who feel as they do and who take pride in safeguarding recipes inherited from their own family or culture.

It takes generation upon generation for a nation's cooking to evolve. English cooking has borrowed from elsewhere for hundreds of years. We took chutneys and kedgeree from India, and before that potatoes, chocolate and tomatoes from the voyages of discovery. Like these ingredients which have now become part of our own cooking, oriental flavours are there in abundance for us to use however we like, and I find it impossible to resist them.

Although in one sense our first visit to Hong Kong marked the real beginning of a deepening interest in oriental food and flavours, the seeds of this book had been sown almost 20 years before that. In the late 1960s my brother, Neil Maloney, went off to Hong Kong where he has lived ever since. Letters were infrequent, visits every couple of years, but I gradually began to learn about oriental ingredients. When he married and brought my sister-in-law and later their children on visits to England, much of our time together was spent in restaurants in Soho's Chinatown, or shopping in

Gerrard Street for what were then exotic ingredients. I can still remember the first meal Bettina cooked for us in our tiny attic flat in Crouch End: noodles, steamed fish, and a clear soup. They were marvellous, fresh flavours. From then on we shopped in Soho from time to time, and I began to incorporate oriental ingredients and techniques into my own cooking. My cookery diary for that week in 1976 shows that soon after Bettina's meal, I cooked a red snapper and steamed it with ginger, spring onions, garlic and soy sauce. The following day I cooked "Chinese vegetables", and on another day steamed courgettes, celery and green beans. I suppose this book began to take shape even then.

After several visits to Hong Kong, I thought it would end there and be a cookery book based on my Hong Kong experiences. But after that I wanted to go in search of "all the Chinas", and travel to wherever Chinese cooks had left their influence. A first short hop to Macau proved fascinating. Not only was there a Chinese culinary tradition but a Western one too, and an Iberian one at that. Then we decided to go to China itself, to Guangzhou because it was close, and on to Shanghai because it was exotic. Next came Taiwan, Thailand, Singapore and Malaysia, and in 1989 I went as guest cook to the Manila Peninsula in the Philippines, which gave me a glimpse into yet another fascinating culinary culture, touched by both Chinese and Iberian influence.

What follows is a collection of recipes based on my own experiments and tastes. I hope it will provide inspiration for others to improvise as I have done. I have interleaved this collection with memories of my travels and food experiences in the Far East. Throughout our travels, we have been offered generous hospitality by individuals and organizations, and have made many good friends. I could not have written this book without them, and if I have missed anyone out of my acknowledgements on p. 6 I am truly sorry.

FRANCES BISSELL

HONG KONG

SHOPPING AND COOKING

Our first visit to Hong Kong in 1986 was about 15 years overdue. We have always allowed Paris, or Venice, or the Loire Valley or New York to get in its way, snobbishly regarding the place as an overgrown duty-free shop. Never were words more happily eaten, along with everything else that was happily eaten in what must be the world's gastronomic capital.

For many people, their first visit to Hong Kong is a short one, in transit to somewhere else. There may be time enough to whizz up to the Peak, ride the Star Ferry, eat in the famous typhoon shelter in Causeway Bay and on one of the floating restaurants in Aberdeen, go to the Poor Man's Nightclub and perhaps even fit in a short visit over the border into China. In the two weeks of our first visit there we didn't manage to do any of these things, except ride the Star Ferry. That was essential transport to get us from one restaurant to another: from Gaddi's at the Peninsula to the Grill at the Mandarin, from the Luk Kwok in Wan Chai to a favourite noodle shop off Nathan Road in Kowloon. Essential transport or not, the Star Ferry is also great entertainment as it chugs across the busy waterway from Hong Kong Island to Kowloon and back, sometimes having to stop engines to allow a bold but ancient sampan right of way. The views of both Hong Kong side and Kowloon side are breathtaking and occasionally we made the trip simply for this, particularly in the early evening when all the brightly coloured unwinking and thus strangely restful lights came on. The Star Ferry is extremely cheap and you get better views if you travel second class because that deck is open.

Despite the thrilling scenery, food was then and still remains our chief preoccupation in Hong Kong. The experience extended beyond eating, as I was lucky enough to be able to cook there and also to shop for food in street markets. Seasons mean very little in Hong Kong. Everything seems to be available all of the time. Strawberries when we were first there came from California, but in a different season might come from Chile or Australia. Mangoes then were from Thailand, small, sweet and fragrant, to be peeled and eaten like bananas. Papayas from the Philippines were, on the other hand, the size of rugby footballs, yet equally full of flavour.

All these were to be found in small general stores in Central, but best of all I liked to explore the steep narrow street full of vegetable stalls leading up to Stanley Street. Here were to be found all manner of green leaves, some local from the New Territories, some from China, and yet others imported from Thailand, Australia and everywhere else which grows something that the people of Hong Kong want. I was particularly taken with the bundles of garlic chives which were just coming into season. Tasting just as their name indicates, these were a great delicacy stir-fried and eaten by the plateful in restaurants and noodle shops.

Opposite the vegetable market in Central is the covered market, for fish, meat and poultry. This is not for the squeamish or the vegetarian. But it was interesting, and brought home to me the insistence on fresh produce, which in Hong Kong means live produce. While I did not feel ready to buy a living bird for my dinner party, I did spend time wandering among the fish stalls. It was colourful, noisy and lively, and I saw fish displayed that I had never seen before, yellow croaker, horse head, rainbow fish, Japanese mackerel, red fish of all types, prawns of every size, some from local waters, some brought in by the deep sea fishing boats from the waters off the Philippines. Everything was weighed in a hand-held balance, by the "catty", something over a pound. I finally decided on sole from Macau and local scallops. The scallops I chose for their beautiful long silver-grey fan-shaped shells, which I had decided to use as decorative serving plates for individual warm fish salads.

In the end I think I preferred Wan Chai market to the Central. Wan Chai is remarkable for the freshness, variety and tempting nature of its produce, the friendliness and good humour of shoppers and stallholders alike. Central is more serious in its fish, meat and poultry, but lacks the picturesque quality of the street market. I went shopping with my sister-in-law Bettina in Wan Chai. She chose her chicken, still live in its cage, the man weighed it and gave her a token. When we left the market she handed in her token and received the chicken, drawn, cleaned and plucked, and in a carrier bag. We also bought prawns and a grey mullet. One stall sold nothing but huge baskets of Tientsin pears in colourful wrappers. Bettina bought several of these, and further on, a big bundle of choy sum. A bunch of gladioli was added. These would get more and more expensive as Chinese New Year approached. Next to the flowers another stall was already selling New Year cards, decorations, flowers and lanterns, all made of red and gold paper.

Further on were piles of water chestnuts, green leaves of many varieties, grapes and pineapples from America, local tomatoes, bananas large and small, taro; pork butchers selling cuts of raw meat, preserved meats and roast pork; preserved meat shops selling sausages, preserved ducks and whole preserved piglets. Then there were baskets of thousand-year-old eggs – grey and white striped and hard to imagine being edible. Pickle shops sold pickled fruit and vegetables, particularly cabbages.

Market trips with my sister-in-law would culminate in domestic Chinese cookery lessons and a lively meal around the family dining table. I was also privileged to be invited into the kitchen of the Fung Lum Restaurant in Shatin by the chef, Chan Fat Chee, who agreed to teach me some Cantonese dishes and techniques. On arriving with our mutual friend George, we were invited to sit down and drink tea with the chef and the owner, and discuss how the day would go. I was to see anything I wanted to see, be taught anything I wanted to learn and to feel completely at home, which I did very quickly. We decided that it would be best for me to learn simple, home-style dishes rather than banquet dishes like salt chicken, which takes two days to prepare. Vegetables and fish were my main interest.

First we all went off to the market. Chan Fat Chee is very well known there and we formed quite a procession with the venerable owner, and George in his shorts, looking like a tourist but speaking impeccably pronounced and nuanced Cantonese, judging by the reactions of those he joked with and from whom he bought roast pork and a giant whelk-like shellfish. We saw all kinds of beancurd, and dried pig's blood, which looked for all the world like chocolate beancurd; tripe, chestnuts, greens, nuts, mushrooms, fruit, fish and meat. Everything was very fresh. The market lacked facilities and a pig was being butchered on the ground, but I would happily shop regularly in such a market. We saw small turtles, which were not wild, but bred specially for the table. We also saw a pig being boned ready to be hung up and dried. I could have stayed there ages, but time was getting on. I had expressed a desire to buy the best dried mushrooms, and we went to a herbalist to get them, as they are considered an important remedy in China. There we also bought ginseng. The oldest roots were extremely expensive (about £150 per ounce), but we were allowed to see and handle them. Ginseng is used in cooking as well as in medicine, and my brother Neil had recently eaten ginseng-stuffed chicken in Seoul.

George bargained for two very large roots and got them for a good price. It pained the proprietor, we were told, but he seemed fairly good-humoured, nevertheless. George also bought some tiny red, raisin-like fruit, which were probably barberries, and then my mushrooms were picked out individually. I clearly got the best: they were a good shape and colour. But I have the feeling that the best-looking, which are also the most expensive, do not always necessarily have the best flavour. There was much else of interest in the shop, including dried deer's penis, powdered horn, and other exotica.

Back at the restaurant, Chan Fat Chee showed us photographs of some very beautiful and ornate imperial banquet dishes he had prepared with relatively inexpensive ingredients, such as egg (the yolk and white cut in different shapes), cherries, melon, pig's tongue, and duck. But as it had taken him a whole day to prepare just one plate, the banquet had necessarily cost a great deal, and in ten years he had prepared only two on such a grand scale.

The kitchen was as I remembered it from a previous visit. The kitchen hierarchy is well established, and everything has its place. I saw how the woks were cleaned immediately after use, felt the relative quiet of the place, inhaled the delicious smells; I noticed the steam cabinet, the flames under the woks, the kitchen boy preparing sea slugs, the cleavers, the chopping blocks simply sliced from tree trunks, and the excellent-looking Yunnan hams hanging up in a dry corner.

First we prepared lunch; Chan Fat Chee showed me how to scrape and peel the whelk, after bashing it open with a hammer on the stone floor of the scullery. Then it was sliced on a ham slicing machine to give paper-thin shavings. It was quickly tossed in chicken stock and wine in a hot wok, then soy sauce and oil were poured over it. We garnished it with chilli, coriander and spring onions. It was delicious. We then prepared steamed garoupa, stuffed beancurd, prawn-filled mushrooms and stuffed broccoli. We fished the garoupa out of the tank in the dining room. Chan Fat Chee stunned it with the flat of the cleaver, scaled it, cut with scissors halfway through the belly then cleaned it through the gills.

I am not quite sure at which point it expired. The fish was placed on an oval dish, on a bed of spring onions; thinly sliced ginger was laid on top and the dish was placed in a drawer of the steaming cabinet for just 10 minutes, after which soy sauce, hot oil and coriander finished it off.

Meanwhile, the beancurd was cut into neat long oblong chunks with a central well scooped out. This was filled with a paste made from raw fish, shredded green vegetables, seasoning and dried orange peel. The beancurd was steamed for 6 minutes and served with soy sauce.

The dried mushrooms were soaked, then simmered for 15 minutes in stock and patted dry. Ah Chan used his fist as a forcing bag and, working with precision, he squeezed a filling into the mushrooms made of pounded raw prawns, cornflour, egg white and seasoning. First, he had sprinkled a little cornflour on to the mushrooms to bind the filling to them, and afterwards, he smoothed over the filling with his thumb dipped in egg white.

After our wonderful lunch, and a rest, I went back into the kitchen to learn how to cook vegetables and to practise the prawn and mushroom dish myself. Ah Chan showed me how to wield two cleavers to pound the prawns, using the backs only to obtain a paste. You know when the consistency is right because it sticks to the blade. I was able to use the wok and scraper and it was tremendous fun.

I learned a lot from Chan Fat Chee and it was a great pleasure to be able to invite him to be my guest for lunch when I was cooking at the Mandarin Oriental. I like to think he enjoyed the food. I know he found it interesting and was most curious about the way in which it was presented. Chan Fat Chee has now left Hong Kong and is cooking in Mauritius. He is a culinary genius, and I miss him on my annual visits to Hong Kong.

HONG KONG

EATING OUT

When it comes to eating out in Hong Kong, it is the contrast that really strikes you, not just the variety. The basic is just a little more basic than anywhere else I know, and the grand just that little bit grander. One night we were treated to a gala dinner at Gaddis, the sumptuous and elegant restaurant at The Peninsula Hotel, which was that year celebrating its 60th birthday. Peter Hatt and his brigade cooked for us freshly sautéed goose liver salad with pink grapefruit and a pomegranate vinaigrette, a heavenly and soothing double-boiled chicken consommé with baby shrimps, grilled scallops in a light soya mousseline sauce, veal mignons with truffled vegetables, pastries, chocolate sorbet and petits fours. The meal was accompanied by exquisite wines, the vintage champagne and the Meursault being particularly memorable. There were just a couple of hints, in the double-boiled consommé and the soya mousseline, that we were in the East.

When I went with the Peninsula's executive chef, Erich Schaeli, and his purchasing manager to have a look at what was available in the local market, I asked him how far his team took the notion of East-meets-West cuisine. The response was interesting and reflected what I was told by most of the chefs and cooks I have met in Hong Kong. All deny that such a thing exists and all emphasize the importance of remaining faithful to their own culinary traditions and training, whether their roots are European or Cantonese. That does not mean to say that they do not experiment: far from it. Hong Kong chefs are innovative and make full use of the rich and varied range of produce to be found on their own doorstep in China, and of the food that comes to them in such profusion from every corner of the globe.

In a stately hotel like the Peninsula the innovations are very subtle. The guests who return here year after year to dine in the restaurant which some still regard as "the finest east of Suez", do not want to be served the sort of "ordinary" food they can eat in any Cantonese restaurant in Kowloon. And yet, some local ingredients, imaginatively used, do find favour. In the market Schaeli chose a bundle of dark hair-like sea moss, "fat tsai", and described how he would use just a little of it to point up a lobster dish with champagne sauce. Peter Hatt takes plump scallops, grills them and serves them with a delicious tomato and soy sauce mousseline. There is just a hint of the exotic but the dish remains firmly within the bounds of classical Swiss French training.

Chef Bokhorst in the Derby Room restaurant at the Happy Valley Racecourse cooked garoupa with Chinese wine, ginger, spring onions, soy sauce and black mushrooms in a most effective dish finished off with a classic beurre blanc sauce which had those extra flavours. At lunch in the chef's office at the Mandarin Oriental, we were served a wonderfully classical meal, terrine of salmon and caviar, duck breasts with mushrooms in a wine sauce and a Sauternes ice cream. But the mushrooms were Chinese and the wine a lovely rich Shaoxing, the Chinese rice wine. People come to Pierrot, the Mandarin Oriental's lovely French restaurant, to eat classical French dishes prepared with style and imagination, as well as a judicious addition of oriental spice. They enjoy such delicacies as veal sweetbreads in a sake and soy sauce with a julienne of crisp vegetables; roast pigeon caramelized with lavender honey and Chinese spices; scallops marinated with lemon juice, fresh mint and sesame oil; and crabmeat consommé flavoured with lemon grass.

Gray Kunz, who used to be chef at the Regent Hotel's Plume restaurant, knew the local markets as well as any of the expatriate chefs in Hong Kong. I remember going with him early one morning on one of the expeditions he used to make at least three times a week. We went to the Nelson Street Market, to Yau Matei and to Sham Shui Po. His daily menu in Plume depended very much on what he found there. Fish, fruit, vegetables, herbs and spices were all sought out with great care. He would use a local fish only if it was highly esteemed in the Chinese kitchen, and therefore he looked for pomfret, garoupa and, as we found that day, mandarin fish, which is a freshwater fish farmed in China. The markets were full of all manner of fresh greens from the New Territories, live chickens and ducks, dried fish, preserved pork, fish swimming in tanks and in buckets, baskets of water chestnuts and bunches of chives.

He particularly looked out for the local seasonal produce that is so highly prized. In spring, there are flat rattan trays of that great delicacy "dao mu", tender pea shoots; in summer, "long-an", a delicate fruit that he served with a chilled fragrant jasmine soup. At

a tea and herb merchant's he bought a bag of dried chrysanthemum flowers and described to me a summery dish in which he
would combine chrysanthemum sorbet and plum soup. Chilled
fruit soups such as mangosteen, and almonds with red wine pears,
were a feature of his daily menu.

I wondered what he was going to do with the mandarin fish,
imagining some oriental delicacy. But Gray Kunz stuck firmly to
classical European cooking. He occasionally used Chinese and
other oriental ingredients, but only after careful experiment had
proved that the flavours and textures would work together. He
was not out to shock. Nevertheless, his dishes were avant-garde to
say the very least; glazed chicken velouté spiced with curry and
lemon grass; mignonette of lamb with taro crust, celery raviolis in a
leek and black bean cream; braised skate fillet with pink basil and
lemon grass butter, and a wonderful cassolette of pea shoots and
fresh Périgord truffles. And the mandarin fish? He filleted it, grilled
it and served it with a thyme butter sauce and a few tiny dice of
vegetables, such as courgettes and red peppers, which gave the
whole dish a very summery, South-of-France flavour.

To help the novice eat Chinese in Hong Kong, the Hong Kong
Tourist Association has excellent publications describing the
different types of Chinese cuisine available, and giving advice on
what and how to order. Everyone you meet will tell you that their
own favourite is "the best restaurant in Hong Kong", but, of
course, there is no such place.

To begin with, you might consider the Chinese restaurants in
the big hotels. The Eagles' Nest at the top of the Hong Kong
Hilton has a marvellous menu and is particularly good if there are
just two of you. You will still be able to enjoy a whole range of
dishes but in smaller portions.

The Victoria Hotel, overlooking the Macau Ferry Terminal, has
a good restaurant called Dynasty. We once enjoyed a rather special
banquet there with several chefs visiting during San Francisco
week, but we also returned on our own one evening and had a
delicious hotpot supper.

Lai Ching Heen at the Regent Hotel is a most beautiful eating
experience. Never before had I been so aware of the importance of
exquisite eating utensils. The place settings are worth a king's
ransom: silver-bound jade plates, jade bowls, jade chopstick rests,
jade and silver napkin rings and ivory and silver chopsticks. The

flowers are always those of the lunar month. The food more than matches the setting. Try to have the celebrated roast "lung kong chicken" and the baked stuffed sea whelk. And do not miss any dish you are offered containing bamboo pith, one of those textural ingredients like shark's fin, bird's nest, jellyfish and sea slug. It is delicious, and its inclusion in a meal means that your host holds you in high esteem.

My favourite "grand" Chinese restaurant is the Man Wah on the top floor of the Mandarin Oriental. On our most recent visit to Hong Kong when I was guest cook at the hotel, we were lucky enough to eat several meals there when I was off duty including one memorable lunch hosted by Jürg Tüscher, the General Manager for Gaston Lenôtre, and some of his associates. We were served all the most highly prized dishes of the Cantonese kitchen, steamed fresh garoupa, shark's fin soup with fresh crab coral, sautéed shredded turtle, and braised abalone and bamboo shoots.

On another occasion, when only four of us lunched, we were served one of their most spectacular dishes. Described as sautéed fillet of sole with vegetable in black bean sauce, the fillets are indeed gently fried and then replaced in the fish skeleton, which has been deep-fried to serve as a crunchy edible container.

The Man Wah is also a restaurant where two can dine quite happily. Put yourselves in Henry's capable hands, tell him of any likes and dislikes and he and the chef will plan a memorable meal for you and will pay you the great compliment of not adapting it to the western taste. Our last meal there included one of my favourite dishes, shark's fin with crabmeat, and we also ate braised Tientsin white cabbage with dao mu (pea sprouts) and conpoy (dried scallops), and a most unusual dish with deep, complex flavours: a deep-fried boneless chicken accompanied by fried Yunnan ham and sweetened walnuts. Dessert was the remarkable double-boiled snow frog and fresh ginseng with red dates and lotus seeds in crystal sugar.

A visit behind the scenes to the Man Wah kitchens goes some way to explaining the high standard of its cooking. It is a most agreeable place to work. Light and airy, with tiled floors and walls, well-stocked fish tanks, room to move between wok section and chopping section, and the whole beautifully decorated with auspicious symbols etched on the windows and walls.

Whenever one discusses favourite Canontese restaurants the

Fook Lam Moon usually crops up. Some say it is the finest Cantonese restaurant in Hong Kong, others say it is overrated. Its importance, however, cannot be overestimated. The owner of the restaurant is in a sense "godfather" to all the fine Cantonese restaurants in the city. Hardly one has opened without a chef who has served his apprenticeship at the Fook Lam Moon. And when a chef moves on it is a serious matter, for he will usually take with him his Number One wok and his Number One chopper at the very least. Then the hotel general manager or restaurant owner will turn to Fook Lam Moon in the hope of finding another chef and a new team waiting in the wings.

Another favourite eating place, right at the opposite end of the scale, is Cheung Kee, a Peking restaurant on Lockhart Road in Wan Chai. It is usually where we go for our first meal out in Hong Kong. Hearing my sister-in-law order the meal is one of the most welcome sounds in the world to us. Going there with a local resident makes it a fascinating experience. Try the dumplings, the onion bread and the fish ravioli. Also particularly good are the roast chicken, the hot and sour soup, and in winter, the hotpot or "da bin lo" dishes.

Our first experience of a Cantonese restaurant came when we were taken out the morning we arrived for a Chinese breakfast of "dim sum" in the large bustling restaurant in the City Hall opposite Queen's Pier. You usually have to wait for a table, so popular is it, but it is worth the wait. Trolleys of steaming bamboo baskets are wheeled endlessly round the room and you stop the waitress if she has something you might like to try. When you choose a basket, a mark is made on the card at your table like a bingo card, and the bill is a simple matter of adding up the number of marks at the end of the meal.

Our favourite place to go and eat dim sum used to be in one of the restaurants at the Luk Kwok Hotel (67 Gloucester Road) in Wan Chai. This was the old-fashioned hotel described by Gavin Young in *Slow Boats Home*. Each time we were there, we were the only Westerners, but we were always made to feel welcome. Some of the waiters spoke English; the amahs who wheeled the trolleys round did not, but nevertheless, we got good service and ate well. Particular favourites were fun gwor (steamed rice flour dumplings filled with pork, shrimp and bamboo shoots), har gau (steamed shrimp dumplings), woo kok (deep-fried yam cakes filled with vegetables), and best of all, see chiu ngau pak yip (steamed tripe in black bean and chilli sauce). The old Luk Kwok was torn down some time ago and a spanking new building rose up in its place, part of which has been re-established as the Luk Kwok hotel.

One of the best places to try Sichuan food is the Sichuan Lau on Lockhart Road, again in Wan Chai. There we ate spicy dishes of sour and peppery soup, fried aubergine in spicy fish-flavoured sauce, delicious onion bread, which is actually more typical of Peking food, and the traditional tea and camphor wood-smoked duck. It was interesting but not, to my taste, as good as it sounds.

Chiu Chow cooking is based on Cantonese cooking and is famous for shellfish dishes and vegetables, all cooked with a light, delicate touch. To experience this, we ventured out alone, without local or Chinese guides, and took ourselves off to the Universal Restaurant in Causeway Bay, opposite the Lee Gardens Hotel. We were directed to a large, bright, busy restaurant on the first floor of a modern block by a receptionist who said: "Only Chinese food. No American food." This was fine by us. As always, when in a strange environment, we watched what the habitúes were doing and ordering. Unfortunately, they were all well into their meal, so we saw no one dealing with the tiny cups of dark liquid. Was it to drink? To wash the chopsticks with? To pour over one's hands? We left it to one side until some newcomers sat down. Of course, by then, the unusual and strong ti kwun yum, a tea also known by the name "Iron Goddess of Mercy", was far too cold to drink.

We ate fried vegetables with conpoy (dried scallops), and minced pigeon and ham, which we wrapped in lettuce leaves, dipped into a vinegary sauce and ate in our fingers. The popular spiced steamed goose, a Chiu Chow speciality, was all gone, but we went on to rice noodles Chiu Chow style, before finishing, much against the maître d'hôtel's wishes, with sweet lotus nuts with white fungus. He did not believe we would enjoy this lovely clear, sweet but not cloying, lemony soup with soft' white nuts and a crunchy, translucent and gelatinous (if something *can* be crunchy and gelatinous at the same time) fungus. We came across this texture again and again, in the jellyfish, which I have heard compared to cold, vinegary rubber bands, and the sea slug, as well as the wood ears, a dark fungus often used in soups and vegetable dishes. This restaurant, and indeed the building, has now gone, but there are plenty of Chiu Chow restaurants in Hong Kong.

Bettina once ordered a marvellous meal for us at a Chiu Chow restaurant, to show us the full range of specialities. We had shark's fin soup, sliced goose with beancurd, thousand-year-old eggs, fried chicken with chingew leaves, satay beef, fried oysters with scrambled eggs, pea shoots (dao mu), and fried noodles Chiu Chow style. The whole meal was delicious. I especially liked the shark's fin soup, which was made with good chicken stock (with the chicken wing still in it), and Yunnan ham as well as shark's fin, with its by now familiar crunchy gelatinous texture. The goose was simply sliced and eaten dipped in vinegar. The eggs were dark grey and soft in the middle, and the whites had turned into a firm dark tea-coloured jelly. They were eaten dipped in sugar or vinegar, or with pink slices of pickled ginger. The eggs are an acquired taste, and we had not quite acquired it.

We were again impressed by the great contrasts to be found when dining out in Hong Kong when we ate at one of its favourite Thai restaurants in Kai Tak road. This is in one of the city's less salubrious areas, and the restaurant was just a few yards from the runway at Kai Tak airport – our table was right on the incoming flight path. Tourists are unlikely to find their way there, so you will find yourself with locals if you do decide to go. The food is very hot, very tasty and very cheap.

Ten of us sat around three rickety red formica-topped tables eating hot, fragrant tom yam (fish soup with the citrusy flavours of lemon grass and makrut, full of prawns and served in a steamboat – a round brass pot with a central chimney), kway tiaw (spicy fried noodles with seafood), pla nueg phad prik (sautéed cuttlefish with fresh chillies), and many more dishes with plenty of rice to absorb some of the chilli heat, and large bottles of beer to quench the thirst. Cutlery and bowls were bright green plastic, "napkins" were sheets torn from the roll of green lavatory paper brought to the table with the cutlery and condiments. Thai food is as fashionable in Hong Kong as it seems to be elsewhere, and the novel table settings only add to the interest.

Dinner in the New Territories was, on reflection, the gastronomic high point of our first visit to Hong Kong, as it has been on subsequent visits. At the Fung Lum restaurant in Shatin, our host George presented us with a menu of fried pigeon, steamed shrimp, stuffed crab claws, steamed garoupa, baked chicken with salt, whole melon with chop suey soup, fried fresh milk, steamed beancurd, sliced beef with green chilli, choy sum with oyster sauce and baked cuttlefish with salt. George had known Chan Fat Chee, the chef who later taught me so much, since the latter was a little boy working in the corner of a restaurant kitchen chopping up vegetables. On entering, George had enquired of the then chef if the crab was fresh. "Oh, yes," insisted the chef. Without a word, the little boy in the corner slowly shook his head from side to side. And they have been firm friends ever since: he had arrived on George's doorstep at eleven o'clock the night before to work out the menu he was to serve us.

Some of the tastes and textures Chan Fat Chee produced were quite new to me. The melon soup, for example. A winter melon was poached, the inside scooped out and filled with a superior soup of chicken, Yunnan ham, roast duck, crab meat, conpoy, duck gizzard and sliced fried mushrooms. The fried fresh milk was milk that had been cooked slowly to evaporate; it had a texture of scrambled eggs and was mixed with fresh crab meat and shredded fried noodles with conpoy sprinkled on top.

Chan Fat Chee once prepared a banquet for fifteen of us, in which we were served the following dishes: steamed shrimp, steamed mushroom with soy, steamed garoupa, baked chicken with salt, mixed seafoods with steamed winter melon, sliced beef with chilli and black bean sauce, green chilli with sliced fish, choy sum with oyster sauce, steamed beancurd, and fried rice. The garoupa was the best I ever tasted: moist, delicate, fresh. The shrimp had that crispness that comes only from extreme freshness. Vegetable carvings – an elaborate bird and a buddha figure – were presented with the garoupa, and I was given these to take home. They take hours to do. The winter melon was also carved, and its message wished us 10,000 good fortunes. Crab, goose, pork, ham and chicken were crammed into the melon with exquisite stock, making a perfect dish for winter. The green chilli was pieces of sweet green pepper stuffed with a minced fish, lemon peel and herb mixture and steamed like the mushrooms. The beancurd and fried rice were perfection. The beef was the least good dish, too long in tenderizer and cornflour according to Bettina.

The banquet lasted three hours and we drank wine with it – a dry white Chennin Blanc. Black Label whisky and Camus XO were also offered, as was an excellent dark tea which I enjoyed instead of the traditional winter jasmine tea.

ORIENTAL FLAVOURS

This chapter is not a comprehensive list of flavours but a selection of ingredients that I consider particularly important in oriental cooking.

FRUIT

CALAMANSI, *calamondin, citrus madurensis, limau kesturi*
This is a small greeny-yellow thin-skinned fruit with many seeds. The flesh is pale yellow. Measuring little more than ¼ inch/2 cm in diameter, with a proportionately small amount of juice, you can imagine how labour-intensive it is to squeeze even enough for one glass of refreshing calamansi juice, a most popular drink in the Philippines. Nevertheless it is used there as much as we in the West use limes or lemons, indeed more so, since soured dishes are a major feature in the Filipino kitchen. It is used for marinating raw fish, for souring meat and fish stews and as a table condiment, to squeeze over fresh fruit for example. It is fragrant, pungent and sharp, with characteristics of both the lime and the lemon, which can replace it. I have seen small limes, known as "limequats", imported from Israel, which can be used in the same way.

COCONUT
Although not used in classical Chinese cooking, the coconut is an important ingredient for flavour and texture throughout Southeast Asia. I use the flesh, the juice or water, and milk and cream made from the grated flesh. It has a natural affinity with fish and shellfish, from mackerel and sardines through squid to crabmeat, prawns and lobster. Use either of the liquids as a cooking medium, as a base for soups and casseroles, or for sweet dishes, creams, custards and ices. The grated coconut flesh is also excellent in the making of sweet baked goods. Occasionally you will find a really fresh one, larger than a football, with a green, shiny skin. Inside is a thick, tough, fibrous husk, then the hard, brittle shell, then the flesh, which may be a layer of thin jelly-like substance in the very immature nut, a thicker creamy flesh or a firm white flesh depending on how ripe it is. It will also contain liquid, which when chilled is a most refreshing drink.

DURIAN, *durio zibethinus*

Do not be put off by all you have heard about the durian being a disgusting thing. It does indeed have a remarkable, strange and to some noses, unpleasant smell but although it smells like hell, it tastes like heaven, as they say in Malaysia. You are likely to come across it during the summer months but it will be very expensive. The hard, khaki-coloured spiky casing, looking for all the world like a medieval battle weapon for swinging round your head and lobbing at the enemy, houses soft, yellow segmented flesh in which are embedded several shiny brown, inedible seeds. The flesh can be made into ice cream or pulped and stirred into a sponge mixture to make a durian cake. A Filipina acquaintance cooks it with chicken, much as I would do with quince or apples. It is best used immediately as its smell will quickly move on to anything else kept in the refrigerator.

JACKFRUIT, *artocarpus heterophyllus*

This is related to the breadfruit which it closely resembles, and is not unlike the durian in internal structure. It is the largest fruit in the world. On the road from Metro Manila to Lake Taal I saw specimens over a yard long and that I would scarcely have been able to put my arms around. The seeds are often toasted and ground for use as a type of flour. The flesh, in a good ripe fruit, is sweet and juicy. It can be cooked or eaten raw.

KAFFIR LIME, *citrus hystrix, makrut, ma krood*

See lime leaves, herb section.

KUMQUAT

The name is taken from the Cantonese for "golden orange". Although not technically a citrus fruit it resembles a small, olive-shaped orange. The whole fruit is edible, with a pronounced, intense orange flavour and fragrance. It does contain many pips however, which are, like orange pips, inedible but a good source of pectin if you wish to make kumquat jam or jelly. The kumquat is much in evidence at Chinese New Year when it is offered as a symbol of prosperity and good fortune. I use it in both sweet and savoury dishes, finding that its fragrance complements fish very well, and its sharp and intense flavour makes it a suitable partner for game dishes.

LONGAN, *dragon's eye*

Somewhat less than an inch in diameter, with a suede-like textured, pale brown brittle skin, the longan is a favourite fruit in Southeast Asia and China. It is very popular in Hong Kong, where it is served in both Chinese and European restaurants. Its sweet, white, juicy translucent flesh is best appreciated raw although it can be used for sorbets and ice creams. In street markets in Kuala Lumpur it is sold by the bunch, a few fruit growing in clusters on each stem. It is available only in late summer and is always looked forward to.

LYCHEE, *lichee, litchi*

About an inch or so in diameter, slightly ovoid in shape, the lychee is one of the most delicious fruits of southeast Asia. Growing mainly in Thailand and Malaysia it is in season during the summer months. The skin or shell is thin and brittle, pinkish brown with a rough surface. It is easiest peeled off with the fingers, revealing a white, opaque fleshy fruit, in the centre of which is a shiny brown inedible seed. The flesh is sweet and juicy with something of the flavour of a muscat grape. Usually eaten on its own after a meal, it is too expensive for me to experiment with in cooking and in any case, heat would destroy its luscious texture and freshness. It does, however, transform into the most wonderful sorbet and ice cream. As an extravagance, you could serve shelled and stoned lychees in a very light syrup, to enhance but not smother the delicate flavour. Although not related, it resembles the longan.

A perfectly ripe lychee has a red or pink skin. If it is underripe, the skin will be greenish or pale beige; if overripe or stored for too long, the skin will be brown.

MANGO

Although we usually have only two or three types at the most to choose from, there are something like 2,500 varieties of mango grown worldwide, tiny heart-shaped yellow ones, slender pale greenish yellow ones which can be peeled and eaten like a banana, pink- and yellow-skinned varieties and dark green-skinned mangoes flushed with red. A ripe mango will give gently, rather like an avocado, when you hold it in the palm of your hand. The flesh is juicy and yellow. Some are more fibrous than others. All have a flat inedible white pit buried in the middle. In the Far East, the mango is made into cooling drinks, ices and desserts. I find it has a natural affinity with chicken, shellfish and smoked foods and like to combine it with these ingredients in mixed salads. Because they are an imported "luxury" item in the West, we are not able to buy them in various stages of ripeness and so we miss out on the delights of the green mango. It can be used as a souring agent, like tamarind pulp, or lemon juice. As well as being a marvellous ingredient for chutneys – like green tomatoes – green mangoes can be grated in salads, used to make refreshing drinks and served, cooked, with fish, rather in the way we might use rhubarb or gooseberries. Try grilled mackerel with a green mango sauce for example.

PAPAYA, *pawpaw*

Rugby football size papayas, cut in half and served with calamansis wrapped in muslin were my favourite breakfast in the Philippines. Ripe, sweet, musky orange flesh, the papaya is hard to beat eaten this way. In Thailand, unripe papaya is grated and mixed with carrots, coriander, lime juice, garlic and spices to make a refreshing salad. The Filipino relish *atchara* is a similar preparation and traditionally served with beef. This makes good dietary sense. Papaya contains the enzyme papain which acts as a meat tenderizer by breaking down the proteins. For exactly the same reason, a papaya sorbet is one of the best things you can serve after a meat-rich meal. A ripe or ripening fruit should have a ring of yellow around the stalk end.

RAMBUTAN

A distant cousin of the lychee, the rambutan is native to Malaysia. You see it being sold in the markets of Kuala Lumpur during the summer months, hanging in bunches. The skin is red-brown or yellowish with soft, hooked spines all over it and can be peeled off with the fingers. The fleshy white translucent fruit is sucked away from the inedible shiny brown stone. It is much too good (and too expensive) to do anything with, except enjoy it as it is.

ROSE APPLE

This is a very pretty, pink waxy-looking fruit which is crisp like an apple and can be eaten in the same way. It is abundant in early spring in the street markets of Taiwan, and is most usually found in a fruit bowl, to be eaten out of hand and not used for cooking.

SAPODILLA

A small, rough-skinned brown fruit very popular in Thailand. It is for the fruit bowl rather than for culinary experimentation, I feel. When ripe the flesh is soft and brown, looks almost overripe but has a caremelly sweetness. The sapodilla is inedible when underripe, full of mouth-puckering tannin. The shiny flat black seeds are inedible. In the unlikely event of your coming across a glut of them, a sapodilla ice cream served with a mango or passion fruit sauce would be a very good combination.

STAR FRUIT, *carambola*

I find this a much more appealing fruit in the tropics than in a Western kitchen. A refreshing drink of iced star fruit pulp is just the thing on a muggy day in K.L., but I can find little use for it in my own kitchen as I do not much like its flavour, which is vaguely reminiscent of that of a pea pod, albeit with a citrusy finish. Its star shape, when sliced, cries out for use as a garnish of course and it is often used in fruit salads.

VEGETABLES

AUBERGINE, *egg plant*

We are all familiar with the deep purple-black, tight-skinned aubergine imported from Holland. In oriental food shops you are likely to come across quite different varieties. Some are small, creamy white and offer an explanation of the vegetable's American name. Others are small, round and a viridian green. Yet others are the size of peas and grow on branching stems. Finger-like *brinjals* with their lilac and white streaked skins are perhaps the most easily recognizable. I like to use them in slow-cooked casseroles but they are also good sliced and fried in hot oil.

BAMBOO SHOOTS

An essential ingredient in many Chinese dishes where they add textural interest rather than a great deal of flavour, fresh bamboo shoots are sometimes found in oriental food shops in the West. If they have already been prepared, they need only to be sliced and boiled. They are an agreeable addition to stir-fried dishes.

CHINESE CHIVES, *flowering chives, garlic chives, kuchai, gau choy fa*

Another seasonal favourite, available in the spring, this is a member of the onion family. The long, hollow angular stems end in small white flower buds and it is usually sold in bunches. In the Chinese kitchen it is cooked as a vegetable and served as a separate dish. I use it as a seasoning ingredient as I might use chives. It does add a most subtle garlicky, oniony flavour to dishes such as omelettes, potato soup, fish dishes and others. I have also used it in risottos (see p. 67) and pasta dishes.

CHINESE FLAT CABBAGE, *taai goo choy*

Growing only a few inches tall, it resembles a flattened stunted bok choy, as its name suggests. It is somewhat coarser in texture but can be used in the same way.

CHINESE FLOWERING CABBAGE, *choy sum*

Its yellowish flowers distinguish this from Chinese kale, and it is slightly more delicate looking. When you see "seasonal green vegetable" on a Chinese menu, flowering cabbage is what you will normally be served.

CHINESE KALE, *Chinese broccoli, gai laan*
This can indeed be cooked and served like broccoli. The firm green stem can be peeled, making it tender and quick to cook when sliced and stir-fried or left whole and steamed. The leaves cook even more quickly. The flower is white and it is best to look for specimens with flowers in bud rather than fully open. The leaves should have a greyish-white bloom to them.

CHINESE LEAF, *Peking cabbage, petsai*
Two types of Chinese leaf are most commonly available, the short barrel-headed variety and the longer, more pointed plant. Both have long, pale, crinkly, tightly wrapped leaves and broad, white stiff stems. It can be sliced and used in salads, sliced and stir-fried or steamed. It has a mild, delicate flavour, without the pervasive cabbagey smell.

CHINESE MUSTARD CABBAGE, *Swatow mustard, gai choy*
With its strong peppery, mustardy flavour this is an excellent vegetable to add to clear soups, or to serve with fish or poultry dishes. Its head resembles that of a leafy green lettuce, but it is also stalky. It is often used to make pickled cabbage, something like an oriental version of sauerkraut.

CHINESE SPINACH, *amaranth, een choy, callaloo*
This is a very widely grown vegetable which you are as likely to find in a Caribbean market as in an oriental one. It is always served cooked and, unlike spinach, I see little to recommend eating it raw. It needs only the briefest cooking times as its broad, dark green leaves are fragile and tender.

CHINESE WATER CHESTNUTS, *ma taai*
Small corms, about 2 inches/5 cm in diameter, water chestnuts have dark brown skin, which can be peeled before or after boiling or steaming, and triangular leaf scales. Choose firm specimens, because the important feature of the water chestnut is not its flavour but its texture. Its crispness is even present when minced and mixed with meat or shellfish fillings wrapped in wonton skins for dumpling soup and it is an excellent ingredient to use if you need to add "bite" to salads and stir-fries. The slightly sweet, nutty flavour makes it suitable for both sweet and savoury dishes.

CHINESE WATER SPINACH, *ung choi*
This is one of my favourite oriental vegetables, a summer treat with green arrowhead leaves. Even though soft and tender, it retains, because of its hollow stem, an agreeable crunchiness after cooking. It has something of the flavour of watercress.

CHINESE WHITE CABBAGE, *pak choi, bok choy, spoon cabbage*
Becoming quite widely available in supermarkets as well as in oriental food shops, this member of the brassica or cabbage family can be recognized by its long white smooth stalks, bunched together like celery from a central root. The leaves are oval, quite thick and fleshy and somewhat spoon shaped. The plants grow to about 15 inches/37.5 cm long and both leaf and stem are edible. Baby bok choy is sometimes available and these are delicious steamed whole and served with a roasted joint instead of broccoli or cauliflower. Shanghai bok choy is similar in shape but the stems are pale green and slightly ribbed.

CORN, *sweetcorn, baby sweetcorn*
Most of us are familiar with the large sturdy ears of corn, husked in pale green, which are so delicious when boiled and eaten hot with melted butter. Small immature yet perfectly formed baby sweetcorn now reaches us throughout most of the year from Thailand. It is a sweet delicate vegetable and is perfectly suited to stir-frying. It can also be grilled or fried and served with fish or chicken. Whole ears of baby corn are sweet and crunchy when eaten raw.

HAIRY CUCUMBER, *fuzzy melon, tseet gwa*
A member of the large cucurbita or squash family, this resembles a small marrow or large courgette, dark green but with a mass of tiny hairs on the skin. It is a type of winter melon, much favoured in Cantonese home cooking as one of those ingredients which soaks up other flavours. It is essential to remove the hairs, which are an irritant. Scrub hard or use a swivel-blade potato peeler to remove the thinnest outer layer of skin.

LOTUS ROOT

The rhizomes of the lotus flower grow under water and resemble a string of stubby fat sausages. The flesh is partly hollow so that when it is sliced, the slices have a decorative lacy appearance. When cooked (which takes about two hours) lotus root retains a good crisp texture which makes it a pleasing addition to a dish of braised meats or mixed vegetables. Lotus root slices are also candied and served as a sweetmeat.

MOOLI, *daikon, white radish*

A long, clean white root vegetable, the mooli adds an agreeable crunchy pepperiness to salad dishes. It is often used in vegetable carvings throughout the Far East. With a relatively high water content, it is best salted and allowed to stand, then rinsed before steaming or boiling.

MUSHROOMS

In the steep street market opposite Hong Kong's Central Market, you will come across deep baskets of straw mushrooms, which are small, clean, round and buff coloured. The fresh oyster mushrooms and shiitake mushrooms now cultivated in Europe can also play a part in oriental-style dishes. Mushrooms, whether fresh or dried and reconstituted, add not only an interesting texture to many dishes but a distinctive flavour. All mushrooms contain glutamic acid, a naturally occurring flavouring related to monosodium glutamate, the white flavouring salt which is gradually falling out of favour with top class oriental chefs and cooks. I would much rather use the flavour-enhancing mushrooms than a chemical powder.

As well as the fresh mushrooms already mentioned, you will come across dried "wood ears" or "cloud ears". These are bracket-like fungi which grow on trees. Sometimes all black, sometimes with a white underside, when soaked they increase enormously in volume. Their texture is at once crunchy and slippery and they make a very good addition to both braised and stir-fried vegetable dishes.

The most expensive of all the oriental mushrooms is the dried Chinese mushroom or flower mushroom, which is the same as the shiitake mushroom. The fresh mushroom is a poor substitute for the deep concentrated flavours of the dried mushroom, which is soaked for 30 minutes before using. The soaking liquid can be used in the finished dish or as the base for another dish. The most prized specimens are the palest buff ones with a white cracked pattern on the top. This opens up like a flower when the mushroom is soaked. Imperfect and therefore less expensive specimens taste as good.

Enoki is the Japanese name for a tiny, thread-like mushroom which is now cultivated in Europe and America. They have little flavour but make a good addition to soups and salads.

ORIENTAL RADISH, *green radish*
More turnip-like than radish-like, this large pale green elongated root vegetable is used as any other root vegetable. It can be mashed, shredded and fried in cakes, or added to soups and family-style casserole dishes. It has a good distinctive flavour.

PEA SHOOTS, *pea tendrils, Holland bean leaves, dao mu*
In season in oriental markets in January and February, these are the slender green topmost shoots of pea plants. Because of their narrow seasonality they are something of a delicacy and are usually served with other expensive ingredients. They wilt very quickly and should be used on the day of purchase, just quickly blanched and then stir-fried. If you grow your own peas in the summer, the tops can be picked for use in the same way.

SEAWEEDS

Although much more common in Japanese cooking, seaweed is used to some degree in Chinese-based cooking. The dried frizzled black hair-like "fat choy" is an important ingredient in Chinese New Year dishes as it is a symbol of long life and good fortune. Its texture when cooked is slippery and gelatinous. Added in very small quantities it makes an interesting ingredient in Western-style butter and wine sauces to accompany fish.

SILK MELON, *loofah, angled loofa, Chinese okra*

A member of the gourd family, this resembles a bent cucumber with ridges, although straight specimens are also available. The ridges and skin can be shaved off with a potato peeler, and the creamy white spongy flesh and slippery seeds can be diced or sliced and added to stir-fries or braised dishes.

WINTER MELON

Despite its name, this is one of the summer squash family. It can be cooked, after peeling, as marrows and courgettes, in soups and vegetable dishes. It comes into its own as a "container" vegetable, when it appears as a course on the banquet table as Winter Melon Pond, the rind beautifully carved in Chinese characters and the "bowl" full of soup that is made of pork, goose, crab, Yunnan ham and stock.

SOYA BEAN

There are so many derivatives of this extraordinary food plant that it deserves a whole section on its own. Who would have imagined that the pale bland creamy beancurd and the dark salty savoury soy sauce have the same origins? This legume produces beans which have a very high protein content. A flour produced from the ground bean is important for those who cannot take gluten, and soya milk is acceptable to those who have a lactose intolerance. The following are the most useful derivatives for cooking.

BEANCURD, *tofu, dao fu*

This is made from soya milk which has been set with a coagulant. Square cakes of white beancurd are available in oriental stores. Kept in water in an airtight container they will last a few days in the refrigerator. Smooth and coarser textures are available. It can be diced, steamed and added to stir-fry dishes. It can be diced or sliced and deep-fried. It can be marinated and then fried or grilled. It can be hollowed out, stuffed and steamed. A "silken" version is used to make soups, dips, "ice creams" and other sweet dishes.

BEANCURD SKINS
Yet another version of the soya bean looks like pale beige thin wrinkled pancakes. Roll the skins around a stuffing and steam or fry them. Shred into strips and add to soups. They can be bought fresh in oriental food shops.

BEAN SPROUTS
Soya beans, and other beans such as mung beans, can be sprouted to the length of an inch or so. These crunchy white, nutty flavoured shoots add an agreeable texture to mixed vegetable dishes and salads.

FERMENTED BLACK BEANS
A marvellous ingredient for braises and slow cooked dishes. Soya beans come in something like 2,000 varieties, many of them grown in China. A black variety is fermented and salted, and the beans are then used, not as a vegetable, but as a flavouring agent. Crushed, they make a marvellous addition to a simple clear sauce for grilled chicken or fish, or to a casserole of lamb shanks or pork.

SOYA SAUCE, *soy, shoyu*
A salty, dark brown savoury liquid derived from fermented, salted soya beans which is used to flavour food. It is excellent in marinades, as a basting liquid and to add a little extra flavour to a stock or a sauce. You will almost certainly not need to add salt. Thin and thick or light and dark sauce is available. In Indonesia a third kind is used, *kecap manis*, a thick sweet sauce, which is marvellous brushed on cutlets before grilling. Black treacle or molasses sugar can be mixed with soy sauce for a similar effect.

ORIENTAL NOODLES
AND
DUMPLINGS

Legend has it that the Chinese invented noodles and that Marco Polo brought them back to Italy from his travels. However, anyone who has visited the *museo storico degli spaghetti* in Pontedassio, Liguria, will be surely convinced that this was not how pasta was introduced to Europe. Thirteenth-century documents in the museums of Genoa and Pontedassio, dated before Marco Polo's return from China, refer to "macceroni" and "lagana". In his own writings, Marco Polo comments that he had eaten "good lagana" in China, indicating that he was already familiar with it. While noodles might not have spread from China to Europe, they certainly spread south and east, and indeed to wherever Chinese cooks went in any number, to Thailand, to Indonesia, to Singapore, to Vietnam, to the Philippines, to Korea and to Japan.

Noodles are made of the staple grain of the region. Thus rice noodles, wheat noodles and wheat dumpling wrappers, buckwheat noodles and noodles made of mung bean flour are all widely used.

It is customary to serve noodles towards the end of a Chinese meal if it is served banquet-style, and not as the Italians do as a prelude to the main course. In serving noodles thus, the Chinese host or hostess is implying that the dishes which have gone before were humble and inadequate and that the guests might now like to fill up with noodles. Of course, one does not do so as this would only serve to confirm that one had not dined well up to this point. I have always regretted seeing those huge bowls of steaming noodles and other good things going back to the kitchen. On less formal occasions, when dishes are served family-style and all put on the table at once, then one can eat one's fill of lovely wheaty noodles. With friends in Hong Kong when we have mixed western and eastern dishes and wines, a bowl of noodles has often been served as a finale and it is a most welcome dish after a meal of rich food and wine.

I like to eat noodles at any time of the day. They make a wonderfully soothing breakfast after a late night out, or a most sustaining quick lunch that will see you through an afternoon of concentrated work. They also make a base for exotic and refreshing salads. A packet or two of dried egg noodles are always to be found in my store cupboard, so that I can make one of the noodle dishes on pp. 64 and 65. Dried noodles will keep well for several months if kept in a dark place in their original packaging. Made from soft wheat flour, rice flour or bean flour, these noodles cook more quickly than pasta. To prepare them it is usual to boil them first then drain and rinse them, before stir-frying or adding to soup. They can also be soaked first and then cooked.

ARROWROOT NOODLES
Traditionally used as soup noodles, they are thin and brittle and sold in bundles.

CELLOPHANE NOODLES, *glass noodles, pea starch noodles*
These are made from mung bean flour. Sold in large bundles, the hard, wiry translucent noodles are soaked in water and absorb four times their weight in liquid. They are often cooked as part of a dish which is then served with rice, unlike the cereal-based noodles. I love to use them cold in spicy, refreshing salads. Harusame are very similar Japanese noodles, made from soya bean flour.

EGG NOODLES
Quite a variety is now available, fresh and dried, broad and narrow, round and flat. The most common of all oriental noodles, egg noodles lend themselves to soups, sauces and fried dishes. Fresh noodles, made like fresh pasta from wheat flour, eggs and water, will keep in the refrigerator for a few days and take only a couple of minutes to cook.

RICE NOODLES, *vermicelli*
Rice noodles are occasionally available fresh, but are usually sold dried. They are opaque and brittle. Use them in soups and also in combination dishes with meat or shellfish and vegetables.

RICE STICKS
These are broader versions of the above, and when fresh look like sticky white ribbons. If fresh, they need to be used within two days. I use them to make my version of guay teow, or Singapore fried rice sticks, an appetizing mixture of noodles mixed with prawns, shredded roast pork, bean sprouts and seasoning.

SHIRATAKI

These are Japanese noodles made from yam flour, recognizable by their gelatinous quality.

SOBA

Japanese noodles made from buckwheat flour, these are thin, round, light brown noodles, not unlike wholewheat spaghetti. These too are very good cold, and make substantial salads.

SOMEN

Threadlike in appearance, these fine white rice flour noodles are added to soups or served as an accompaniment to meat dishes in Japanese cooking.

UDON, *udong*

Made from wheat flour and water, these Japanese noodles are flat and ribbon-like.

WONTON, *dumplings*

Like the *pelmeni* of Siberia and *mamocha* of Nepal, this is the Chinese version of ravioli. Sometimes available ready filled, it is also possible to buy the wonton wrappers fresh or frozen. These are made from a thinly rolled paste of wheat flour and water, cut into 3 inch/7.5 cm squares. Traditional wontons might be filled with pork or shrimp or a mixture of pork, shrimp and mushrooms and served in a broth as wonton soup, or the dumplings might be steamed and served as a snack or "dim sum". One of my favourite versions is on p. 86, filled with a spicy salmon mixture and served as an hors d'oeuvre. But there is no reason why you should not fill them with sweet things and serve them as a pudding.

YIFU NOODLES, *efu noodles or yi noodles*

One of my most memorable breakfasts consists of a bowl of yifu noodles, some pickles, a pot of po lih tea and a glass of soya milk served to me at a floor length window 30 storeys up in the Shanghai Hilton. Yifu are almost instant noodles, sold in dried, woven, round "cakes". They are pre-cooked. Use them for soups and stir-fries.

HERBS, SPICES

A few key flavours underpin the food of Southeast Asia and, when I look back, these were the ingredients which I found the most appealing and tempting and which I couldn't wait to use in ideas of my own. Ginger, galangal, fresh turmeric, lemon grass, lime leaves and star anise have become, whenever I can get them, an important part of my cooking. Basil and coriander had long been among my favourite herbs and after encountering them in quite unfamiliar dishes in Thailand, I began to see them in a much wider role.

ANNATTO, *achiote, asuete*

The seeds of a tropical tree, annatto is used in the Philippines, as a legacy of the Spanish colonial period, largely as a colouring and flavouring, for lard and other cooking fats. In Europe it is also used as a dye for various foodstuffs such as cheese and smoked fish.

BASIL, *holy basil*

Holy basil is an important flavouring in Thai cooking and although it can be bought occasionally in oriental stores, fresh sweet basil can be used as a substitute. It adds a lovely, warm fragrance of spices and particularly of cloves, although holy basil has more of a hint of anise, and you can also find a cinnamon basil and a spice basil, not to mention lemon basil. It goes particularly well with shellfish, vegetable and salad dishes.

CASSIA, *Chinese cinnamon*

Like cinnamon, this is the dried bark of an evergreen tree, sold in pieces or powdered form. It does not have quite the same delicate flavour of cinnamon and is best reserved for savoury dishes. It is one of the ingredients of Chinese five-spice powder.

CHILLI, *chilli peppers*

Although a vegetable, these hot spicy little pods are used as a seasoning and thus I feel their proper place is in this section. The seed pod of a plant of the same family as the familiar sweet red and green peppers, chillies can have a devastating effect unless they are used with care.

Almost every rule you have heard about chillies has exceptions. The pointed ones are supposed to be the hottest, but then I was sent some small blunt green ones from St Helena on Ascension Island, and told to beware, these were the hottest possible. I have to say that I am not fond enough of chillies to test them against the tiny red and green bird peppers of Thailand which I have seen people eat raw, as one might munch an olive, and which are also said to be the hottest. Whichever chilli you choose, assume it is extremely hot until proved otherwise.

Capsaicin, the bitter alkaloid contained in chillies, is very volatile. Wash your hands thoroughly after contact, or wear rubber gloves. Bathe eyes and mouth in cold water if they are inadvertently touched with raw chilli. To take out some of the heat, split the chilli down the middle and remove stalk end and seeds. Some say that the tip is the hottest part and you may want to remove this too. All these warnings apart, chillies do add a certain something and are an important flavouring in the Far East.

CHINESE FIVE-SPICE POWDER
As with garam masala of India and the ras el hanout of Morocco, this is a combination of spices. In this mixture, however, the combination is constant and does not change according to the cook's task. The ingredients are anise pepper, cassia, fennel seeds, star anise and clove, all ground to a fine brown powder. The scent and flavour is distinctly that of anise. Use it in small quantities, in marinades and basting liquids as well as in stocks and casseroles. Use too much, however, and your dish will take on an almost liquorice flavour.

CORIANDER

One of the other names of this pungent and exotic herb is Chinese parsley. It does indeed slightly resemble flat leaf parsley, with its glossy green serrated leaves. Leaves, root, seeds and flowers can all be used. I find it particularly good with pork dishes and fish dishes.

FENNEL SEEDS

The delicate anise/liquorice flavour to be found in these seeds makes them a useful substitute for five-spice powder or star anise.

GALANGAL, *galingale, Laos root, lengkuas*

A rhizome like ginger, this has something of the flavour of ginger, but is somewhat milder. It is available as a fresh root, a dried root or in powdered form. Ginger is more commonly available and is an excellent substitute in dishes that have either a Malaysian or a Singaporean flavour.

GINGER

Available as a young fresh root or rhizome, as "green ginger", as a drier, older root, or of course in powdered or crystallized form. Look for the firmest specimens possible, with a tight satiny skin and few protruberances. It is a favourite ingredient in my cooking, in sweet and savoury dishes alike. I insert slivers of fresh ginger under the skin before I roast a duck, or chop it into a stuffing for fish or chicken. It is also excellent for flavouring sweet rice puddings and ice creams.

If you find a very fresh piece with healthy looking shoots break a couple off and pot them in standard potting compost. You may be lucky enough that it will grow into a beautiful ornamental houseplant. And as a bonus it will give you a new fresh rhizome, although you have to destroy the plant to get at it of course.

GINSENG

A root to which many myths and legends are attached, including that of the power to raise from the dead those who eat it, this is an important plant in oriental medicine. And because foodstuffs are chosen for their healing properties, in the case of illness ginseng also finds its way into the oriental kitchen. Young and old roots are available in all manner of grades. The Korean grading system refers to some ginseng as "earth" and the better ones as "heaven" (better meaning older and thus more potent). I have learnt from Chinese cooks how to make a ginseng chicken, which is an excellent dish, even if you feel perfectly healthy. The forked root, perhaps 5 inches/12.5 cm long, will be slightly wrinkled and dry to the touch and pale brown or sandy fawn. It is not necessary to peel the root before putting it in the pot. Ginseng has a pleasant earthy, slightly sweet taste and the whole root can be cut up and shared after it has been cooked.

Ginseng is in an anomalous position, not being recognized by the British Pharmacopoeia, but being banned as an illegal substance by the International Olympic Committee.

If the body is any way under stress then ginseng helps it to repair itself. In a healthy unstressed body, however, it has little noticeable effect.

LEMON GRASS

An intensely lemony fragrance is added to any dish by the judicious use of a piece or two of lemon grass. You can get something of the same effect by using zest of lemon, or better still, a leaf or two of lemon balm. Lemon juice is no substitute at all since it has no fragrance and lemon grass has no sourness. The part of the plant that is used is the tightly furled leaf shoot just above the root. It can be sliced, or used whole to scent steam or infuse a liquid. Dried lemon grass is available, both whole and rubbed in tiny pieces.

LIME LEAVES, *ma krood, makrut*

This aromatic leaf is one of the most distinctive flavours of Southeast Asia and it is easy to recognize in the shops, looking like a figure of eight with two leaves joined together end to end. Just a couple of leaves tucked around a joint of lamb before roasting perfumes it in the way that a sprig of rosemary does. The leaves also make an excellent addition to fish or shellfish soups and stews.

PANDANUS LEAF, *pandan*

This long slender spiky leaf of the screw palm has a warm fragrance and delicate flavour which I like to apply to milk puddings. Crushing the leaf will produce a green colouring originally used for such dishes as the Malay *kueh* or cake, although synthetic food colouring is now very often substituted.

SZECHUAN PEPPERCORNS, *far chiu*

These are the dried seeds of the prickly ash tree. In Japan, the leaf of the same tree is used to make Japanese fragrant pepper or *sansho*. The small reddish brown seeds are indeed aromatic when dry-fried, ground and sieved. I find that they have a curious mouth-numbing quality.

TAMARIND

This dark brown sticky pulp is scraped from the pods of a tropical tree. It is usually sold in blocks from which pieces are broken off as required and soaked in hot water to produce an astringent liquid. It is an important ingredient in the Philippines where there are words in the various languages which denote the degrees of sourness tamarind provides. It is also added to curries in Thailand and other parts of the continent. Other agents such as wine vinegar and lemon juice do not have the same effect because they lack the distinctive flavour of tamarind. A fine balsamic vinegar perhaps comes closest with its mellow richness.

TURMERIC

A small rhizome of the ginger family, it has bright orange flesh and, when fresh, a mildly spicy flavour which makes it an excellent addition to a range of fish and light meat dishes.

OILS

GROUNDNUT OIL

The most popular oil for oriental cooking is groundnut, or peanut oil. It is a pale, clear, neutrally flavoured oil that, like refined olive oil, withstands very high temperatures, up to 200°C/400°F. (All other oils should be used at lower temperatures.) This heat tolerance makes it ideal for use with both the domestic wok and the powerful gas-fired wok found in restaurant kitchens. The critical point for oils, when they begin to break down and release the toxin acrolein, is when they smoke. Groundnut oil is less likely to reach this point. The oil can be reused up to 10 times if carefully filtered each time. If the oil does reach smoking point, it must be discarded. Groundnut oil also remains liquid at normal refrigerator temperature, although it is not necessary to keep it refrigerated.

SESAME SEED OIL

Two types of sesame oil are sold. One is a pale, clear oil, with a sweetish flavour, that keeps well. This is virgin sesame oil from a cold pressing of the seeds. The oil used in oriental cooking, also called seasame oil or sesame seed oil, is pressed from toasted sesame seeds and is a rich clear brown with a distinctive nutty flavour. It is not used as a cooking medium because it has a low smoking point, but added at the end to flavour food. I use it to marinate raw fish as well as to sprinkle on grilled or steamed fish.

VINEGARS

Whilst classic Western vinegars such as wine vinegar and cider vinegar can be used in oriental-style dishes, it is nice to use the authentic ingredients if you can get them. If not, then I find that sherry vinegar makes a good substitute for rice vinegar, and sherry itself an acceptable alternative to mirin, sake or the other rice wines. But there are even more exotic vinegars, particularly in the Philippines where sour dishes are a major feature of the cuisine.

COCONUT VINEGAR
This thin opaque white liquid is made from fermented coconut juice. It is used as a souring agent in Filipino cooking.

PALM VINEGAR
This is made from the fermented sap of the palmyra palm, from which a potent palm wine and a clear strong spirit are also derived. It is widely used in Filipino cooking.

RICE VINEGARS
These are made, like other wine vinegars, from soured and fermented rice wine. The vinegars from China are sharp and extremely sour. Those from Japan, particularly brown rice vinegar, are mellow, rounded and almost sweet.

STARTERS

TOMATO AND GINGER ICE
With VODKA

This is an unusual and refreshing starter which can also be served as a chilled soup if the idea of a sorbet does not appeal. I do not recommend serving it as a between-courses sorbet as the flavours are powerful and will impose on rather than cleanse the palate.

Serves 6-8

900 g/2 lb ripe tomatoes
   30 g/1 oz freshly grated or sliced ginger
   75 ml/3 fl oz water
   1 tsp salt
   1 tsp sugar
   • several grinds black pepper
   1 tsp Angostura bitters
   1 tsp Worcester sauce
   1 tsp soy sauce
   • celery leaves, or fennel or dill fronds
   • vodka to taste

Cook the tomatoes and ginger very gently for 5 minutes with the water, sugar and salt. Process and sieve. Allow the purée, or rather, thick juice to go cold. Season with pepper, bitters and the two sauces, but check for taste as you may wish to add more.

Freeze the liquid in an ice cream maker according to the directions, or in a container in the freezer. If using the latter method you will need to stir it from time to time once it has begun to freeze to break down the ice crystals. The food processor is handy for this and gives the resulting ice a good texture.

Serve the ice, slightly ripened in the refrigerator, in glass tumblers, garnished with some tender celery leaves or fronds of dill or fennel, and pour a small measure of good quality, chilled vodka over each.

CHICKEN AND COCONUT SOUP With RICE NOODLES

This is based on that delicious Malaysian dish, "laksa". It is soothing and satisfying and makes an excellent lunch or supper dish. The spicy sauce or sambal can be made in quantity and kept in the refrigerator.

Serves 6

SPICY SAUCE

4 shallots or 1 medium onion,
  peeled and finely chopped
8 garlic cloves, peeled and crushed
6 tbsp groundnut oil
4 dry chillies, soaked and chopped
140 g/5 oz ripe tomatoes,
  roughly chopped
1 tsp sugar
1 tsp ground coriander seeds
1 tsp ground cumin seeds

Gently fry the shallots and garlic in the groundnut oil until soft. Add the rest of the ingredients, bring to the boil, cook for a few minutes and rub through a sieve. Put in a bowl and cover until required.

SOUP

170 g/6 oz thin rice noodles or vermicelli
225 g/8 oz chicken breast meat
570 ml/1 pint chicken stock
570 ml/1 pint coconut milk
15 g/½ oz tamarind paste,
  or 2 tbsp lemon juice
15 g/½ oz grated fresh ginger
4 kaffir lime leaves,
  or 1 piece lemon grass
3 tbsp shrimp paste
200 g/7 oz prawns
85 g/3 oz bean sprouts
85 g/3 oz peeled, seeded
  and chopped cucumber

Blanch the noodles in boiling water for 3-4 minutes, drain and refresh under cold water and put to one side. Poach the chicken breast for 8 minutes, remove and when cool enough to handle, shred it and put to one side. Put the stock and coconut milk in a large saucepan, add the tamarind, ginger, lime leaves and shrimp paste. Bring to the boil and simmer for 5 minutes. Add the prawns, chicken, bean sprouts, cucumber and noodles. Bring to the boil and serve immediately, either in individual soup plates or in a large tureen from which everyone can help themselves. Hand round separately a small dish of fried onion rings, one of sliced chillies, one of fresh coriander leaves and one containing the sambal or spicy sauce.

CHILLED CARROT
AND MANGO SOUP

Despite the oppressive heat and humidity of the summer months, chilled soups are not popular in Southeast Asia. Hot soups are still the norm, but made with "cooly" rather than "heaty" ingredients. "Cooly" food includes fish, mushrooms and vegetables. Food that heats you, and thus "heaty" food, as it is described in Singapore, includes most of the meats. What cools me best however, is a silky chilled soup, slightly spicy, slightly fruity and with a hint only of sweetness.

Serves 6-8

    2 tbsp sunflower oil
    1 onion, peeled and chopped
    1 celery stalk, trimmed and chopped
    1 potato (85 g/3 oz) peeled and diced
340 g/12 oz carrots, peeled and diced
    2 tsp cumin seeds
  • seeds of 6 cardamom pods
1.75 l/3 pints vegetable or chicken stock
    1 ripe mango
    1 tbsp chopped chives

Heat the sunflower oil, and fry all the vegetables and spices until the onions are golden brown. Pour on half the stock, and cook until the vegetables are soft. Allow to cool, and transfer to the bowl of a food processor. Peel the mango, and slice the flesh into the food processor. Blend until smooth, and seive into a glass serving bowl or tureen. Stir in the rest of the stock, and chill until required. To serve, garnish with chopped chives and, if you wish, some single cream or yogurt.

DUMPLING SOUP

The familiar wonton soup of the Chinese kitchen is also a traditional Filipino dish known as *pancit molo*. If you have a ready supply of wonton wrappers it is a very good idea to make a large batch and keep them until required. The combination of chicken, pork, ham and prawns is the authentic version, though one or two of these main ingredients would suffice.

Serves 6-8

    1 onion
    1 carrot
    1 celery stalk
    6 water chestnuts or a
       Jerusalem artichoke
  85 g/3 oz lean boneless chicken
  85 g/3 oz lean boneless pork
  85 g/3 oz cured lean ham or bacon
  85 g/3 oz peeled prawns
    2 tbsp soy sauce
    1 tbsp sesame oil
  30 wonton wrappers
1.75 l/3 pints chicken stock

Peel, trim and roughly chop the vegetables, and put in a food processor together with three-quarters of the meat and prawns. Dice the rest and reserve. Process the meat, prawns and vegetables with the soy sauce and sesame oil until you have a smooth paste. Spoon a little filling into each wrapper, wet the edges, and draw together to make a bundle. Pinch together to seal it. Bring the stock to the boil, and drop in the dumplings and the reserved diced meat and prawns. Bring back to the boil, simmer for 8-10 minutes and serve very hot.

CLEAR TURKEY SOUP

*T*ry to resist the temptation of putting too many different vegetables into the soup. Made with six vegetables, it is definitely not twice as good as made with three. The same recipe can be adapted to other stocks: chicken, salmon, beef or shellfish.

Serves 6

1.45 l/2½ pints clear, richly flavoured turkey stock
1 lemon grass stalk, sliced
6 baby leeks, thinly and diagonally sliced (1 or 2 adult leeks will suffice)
9 baby sweetcorn cobs, split in half
6 cherry tomatoes, seeded and quartered
● fresh coriander leaves

Put the stock into a saucepan and bring it to the boil. Drop in the lemon grass and leeks and simmer for 2 minutes. Add the sweetcorn and tomatoes and cook for 2 minutes more. Put the coriander leaves into soup bowls and ladle the boiling soup on top. Serve immediately. If you have any, stir in a couple of tablespoons of shredded *raw* turkey or chicken with the sweetcorn. Adding cooked meat is not a good idea as it diminishes the fresh flavours of the soup.

To turn this into a substantial lunch dish, prepare some noodles as described on p. 61 and serve them in a large bowl topped up with the soup.

SUMMER BEANCURD SOUP

Serves 4-6

60 g/2 oz mangetout
85 g/3 oz oyster mushrooms
6 baby corn cobs
1 lemon grass shoot
1 packet silken tofu
1.15 l/2 pints chicken or vegetable stock
1 tbsp basil, shredded by hand
● salt, pepper

Top and tail the mangetouts. Leave them whole if they are small, otherwise cut into three or four pieces diagonally. Tear the oyster mushrooms into wedges, or leave them whole if small. Slice each corn cob in two lengthways. Slice the lemon grass into several pieces. Drain the tofu and cut into 1 cm/½ inch cubes. Carefully put all these ingredients into a saucepan of simmering stock. Let it cook for 3-4 minutes, stir in the basil, season to taste and serve immediately. A few peeled prawns, sliced scallops or slivers of sole or plaice could be added to the soup, in which case you might choose to use fish stock.

SCALLOP AND COCONUT SOUP

Avery delicate soup, easy and quick to cook. You need to have all the ingredients to hand and prepared before you start cooking. For a more elaborate dish, serve it with the coral dumplings.

Serves 4-6

- 1 piece lemon grass
- 2 lime leaves
- 4 sprigs fresh coriander
- 2 star anise pods
- 6 peppercorns
- 570 ml/1 pint light chicken, vegetable or shellfish stock
- 570 ml/1 pint coconut milk
- 3 tbsp shredded fresh coconut meat
- 8 prepared scallops, white meat only, cut in half across (use the corals for the dumplings)
- 85 g/3 oz garlic chives, cut into 3 inch/7.5 cm lengths
- fresh coriander leaves
- salt to taste

Put the herbs, anise and peppercorns in the chicken stock, bring to the boil, simmer for 5 minutes, remove from the heat and infuse for 30 minutes. Strain into a clean saucepan, add the coconut milk and coconut meat and bring to the boil. Poach the scallops in the liquid for 2 minutes, adding at the same time the garlic chives and coriander. Season to taste, and serve immediately. If you are serving the soup with the coral dumplings, they should be poached in the broth with the herbs for 5 minutes or so before you add the scallops.

CORAL DUMPLINGS

Makes 12

- coral from 8 scallops
- 1 tsp fish sauce or shrimp paste
- 60 g/2 oz silken tofu
- 15 g/½ oz peeled fresh ginger
- 2-3 cloves garlic, peeled
- 1 tsp soy sauce
- dash of Tabasco
- pinch of ground Szechuan pepper
- 12 wonton wrappers

Blend all the ingredients until smooth. Spoon on to the wonton wrappers, moisten the dough round the filling, and draw it together over the filling, pinching it to seal it. To cook, poach in boiling stock, soup or water, or steam them. Serve in soup, or with a dipping sauce, see p. 60.

Overleaf: Scallop and Coconut Soup;
Coral Dumplings; Dipping Sauce (p. 60)

WINTER BEANCURD SOUP

Serves 4-6

110 g/4 oz pork tenderloin
110 g/4 oz chicken breast
1 shallot, peeled and thinly sliced
1 tsp groundnut oil
1.15 l/2 pints chicken or
    vegetable stock
170 g/6 oz broccoli florets
1 tbsp cornflour
1 packet silken tofu
1 tbsp coriander leaves
1 egg yolk, lightly beaten
• salt, pepper

Cut the meat into narrow (5 mm/¼ inch wide) strips and fry with the shallot in the groundnut oil for 5 minutes over a moderate heat, stirring to stop the ingredients burning. Pour on the stock, bring to the boil and simmer for 5 minutes more. Add the broccoli florets and simmer for 2-3 minutes. Mix the cornflour to a smooth paste with a little cold water and stir into the soup. Cook it for a further minute or two before adding the tofu cut into small squares, and the coriander. Bring the soup to simmering point and stir in the egg yolk until it sets in threads. Season and serve. For those who like hot and spicy soups, a chilli or two could be shredded into it.

TURKEY WONTONS

This makes a delicious appetizer to serve over the festive season. If you serve them with a clear turkey soup (p. 48), you have a marvellous starter for Boxing Day, so good that people will never imagine you are using up leftovers.

Makes 24

1 turkey liver
1 tbsp groundnut oil
3 spring onions or baby leeks
85 g/3 oz bean sprouts
2 cloves garlic, peeled and crushed
2.5 cm/1 inch piece of fresh ginger,
    peeled and grated
2 tbsp soy sauce
1 tsp clear honey
2 tsp rice vinegar
60-85 g/2-3 oz cooked turkey meat
24 wonton wrappers

Trim any sinews and discoloured parts from the liver, slice it and fry it in the groundnut oil for 2-3 minutes. Put it to one side. Trim the onions or leeks and chop or slice them finely. Chop the bean sprouts. Mix the vegetables with the garlic and ginger and then the soy sauce, honey and vinegar. Mix in the turkey meat. Finely chop the liver and add this to the mixture. Taste to check the seasoning. Spoon a little into the centre of the wonton wrapper, dampen the edges and pinch it together to seal it. Fill the rest in the same way. The wontons can then be deep-fried, steamed or simmered in soup.

MARINATED MACKEREL
IN
LIME JUICE
AND
COCONUT MILK

The texture and flavour of very fresh raw mackerel, just lightly marinated, is quite exceptional. I much prefer it to cooked mackerel. I first tasted a marinade similar to this with fresh sardines in Paris at Michel Oliver's Bistro de Paris. Farmed salmon, rainbow trout or fresh fillets of plaice would be worth trying. Fresh coconut juice is essential, not the processed coconut milk or cream.

Serves 4

- 1 coconut
- 4 mackerel fillets
- • sea salt
- • black pepper
- 2 tbsp groundnut, sunflower or other oil with a neutral flavour
- 2 limes
- • salad leaves for serving, optional

Extract the juice from the coconut and pour it into a jug. Crack the nut and with a sharp knife, zester or cannelling knife remove strips or curls of coconut flesh to garnish and flavour the dish, about 4 tablespoons should do it. Slice each mackerel fillet into 3 long diagonal slices, as if you were slicing smoked salmon. In thin slices like this the fish will marinate quickly. Arrange in a single layer in a flat dish. Sprinkle lightly with sea salt and freshly ground black pepper and pour on the coconut juice. Leave for 20 minutes then dribble the oil over the fish, brushing it all over to make sure that each slice is covered. Remove a few shreds of zest from one lime, for garnish, then cut it in half. Squeeze the juice all over the fish and, with a wooden spoon so the slices are not torn, gently stir to coat thoroughly. Arrange on four individual plates, with or without salad leaves. Garnish with coconut and lime shreds and serve with the other lime, cut into quarters.

Overleaf: Marinated Mackerel in Lime Juice and Coconut Milk

SALADS
AND
ACCOMPANIMENTS

CRABMEAT
AND
QUAIL EGG SALAD
With
WARM TOMATO VINAIGRETTE

Serves 4

- 1 dozen quail eggs
- mixed salad leaves
- 170 g/6 oz fresh white crab meat
- 170 g/6 oz ripe skinned tomatoes or drained canned tomatoes
- 1 clove garlic
- salt
- freshly ground black pepper
- 1 tbsp rice or sherry vinegar
- chives or garlic chives

Put the quail eggs in cold water. Bring to the boil, simmer for 30 seconds. Run under cold water and shell them carefully. Arrange the salad leaves on four individual plates, divide the eggs between them, together with the crab meat. Heat the tomatoes gently for 5 or 6 minutes, without letting them get too hot, together with the garlic, seasoning and vinegar. Rub the mixture through a sieve and spoon it around, but not over, the salad. Garnish with lengths of chives.

VEGETABLE PLATTER
With
GINGER TOFU DIP

This is simply a plate of crudités, as carefully and elegantly prepared as possible, served on a bed of cracked ice with a delicious and unusual dip made from tofu – soya beancurd. It has a creamy texture and little flavour of its own but makes the perfect base for a herb cream.

Serves 4

- 110 g/4 oz silken tofu
- 1 shallot
- 2 tsp freshly grated ginger
- 2 cloves garlic
- 2 tbsp chopped garlic chives or chives
- salt, pepper

Put all the ingredients in the blender or food processor and process until smooth.

Serve with raw vegetables. This also makes an excellent sauce to accompany cold fish, shellfish or chicken dishes.

SESAME SALAD

For this dish, choose a variety of crunchy vegetables which you can quickly prepare. I like to use the ones suggested below.

Serves 4

110 g/4 oz Jerusalem artichokes
110 g/4 oz Brussels sprouts
110 g/4 oz carrots
110 g/4 oz bean sprouts
110 g/4 oz red cabbage
  4 tbsp apple juice
  2 cloves garlic, optional
  2 tbsp toasted sesame oil
  1 tbsp soy sauce
  2 tbsp toasted sesame seeds

Working quickly, trim, wash, slice or shred the vegetables as appropriate. With the Jerusalem artichokes, I find they are best peeled and sliced wafer-thin, or shredded. Sprinkle them with some of the apple juice to keep them pale. Arrange the vegetables on either individual plates or one platter, perhaps in wedges of colour. Mix the garlic, sesame oil, remaining apple juice, soy sauce and sesame seeds, pour over the vegetables and serve immediately.

Sunflower seeds and oil can be substituted for the sesame seeds and oil.

MARINATED SQUID SALAD

This dish would look very attractive served in half coconut shells if you were able to collect enough of them. Do it perhaps when you have bought a couple of coconuts to make the dishes on p. 46 or p. 49.

Serves 4-6

455 g/1 lb small arrow squid
  2 tbsp groundnut oil
1-2 cloves garlic, peeled and
      finely chopped
100 ml/3½ oz coconut juice
  1 tbsp calamansi or lime juice
  • salt, pepper

GARNISH

60 g/2 oz fresh coconut meat,
    cut into shreds
  1 lime, sliced or cut into wedges
  • fresh coriander leaves

Wash and clean the squid. Slice into thin rings and fry in the oil together with the garlic. Cook for just 2-3 minutes until the squid is tender but still firm. Drain and put in a bowl. Add the coconut and calamansi or lime juices and season with salt and pepper. Chill until required. Arrange on a single serving plate or individual plates and garnish with shredded coconut meat, wedges or slices of lime and coriander leaves.

MUSSEL AND CELERIAC SALAD

The first time I wanted to make this salad for the Clipper Lounge in the Mandarin Oriental in Hong Kong, I was asked if I would not mind using oysters instead. In Hong Kong oysters were more readily available than mussels, but I give the original recipe here as it seems more practical. You could, of course, use a mixture of shellfish. Do not be tempted to use ready-cooked mussels in brine or vinegar. The briny, sweet iodine flavour of fresh mussels is a marvellous complement to the nutty, earthy sweetness of the celeriac.

The ginger and coriander dressings also go very well with root vegetables. Try either with a dish of boiled sliced carrots served just warm for starters.

Serves 4-6

340 g/12 oz peeled celeriac root
    1 tbsp lemon juice
900 g/2 lb live mussels
    8 coriander stalks and leaves
  • ground white pepper
    4 cm/1½ in piece fresh ginger

FOR DRESSING 1

3 tbsp sunflower oil
1 tsp sesame oil

FOR DRESSING 2

4 tbsp homemade mayonnaise

Thinly slice the celeriac and cut into julienne strips. Drop them as you go into a pan of cold water with the lemon juice. Bring to the boil, hold there for about half a minute, drain and refresh under cold water. Put the celeriac to one side. Scrub the mussels under the cold tap to remove any sand. Knock off any barnacles with the back of an old knife and tug off the byssus or beard. It comes away easily enough if you pull it down the length of the shell. If any mussels remain open after this vigorous treatment, discard them. Give them a final rinse and put them in a lidded saucepan. Wash the coriander and put the stalks in with the mussels, chopping the leaves and reserving them for decoration. Grind some pepper over the mussels. Peel and grate the ginger, putting the peel in with the mussels and the grated flesh to one side. Put the lid on the mussels and set them over a high heat. Steam them in their own juices until they just open, about 2-3 minutes is usually enough. Tip the mussels into a colander set over a bowl to collect the juices. When the mussels are cool remove them from their shells and put them in a bowl with the celeriac. Mix them by hand.

DRESSING 1, mix 2-3 tablespoons mussel liquor with the grated ginger, and the oils. Whisk to amalgamate all the ingredients and stir in the reserved chopped coriander. Carefully mix into the celeriac and mussels.

DRESSING 2, mix 2-3 tablespoons mussel liquor with the mayonnaise and stir in the ginger and reserved chopped coriander. Mix into the celeriac and mussels.

Let the salad stand covered for 30 minutes before serving for the flavours to develop.

CHICKEN, MANGO
AND MUSHROOM SALAD

This is a simple, eye-catching dish, with a very appealing combination of flavours. I have served it in Hong Kong and in Manila, where it was very popular. One day, one of the Filipino chefs added a few smoked oysters to the dish, which was a very good addition.

Serves 4-6

2-3 boneless chicken breasts
1-2 fresh ripe, but firm, mangoes
225 g/8 oz fresh mushrooms
1 tsp mustard
1 tbsp calamansi or lime juice
4-5 tbsp olive oil
• salt, pepper

GARNISH

• blanched broccoli florets, fresh herbs or spring onion brushes

Remove the skin from the chicken breasts and poach or steam them for 8-10 minutes. Cool them quickly and then chill them to make slicing easier. Slice into long, neat slices. Peel and slice the mango. Wipe and slice the mushrooms if they are large, or leave whole if small. Blanch them quickly in boiling water and drain them. Arrange the chicken, mango and mushrooms on a single serving plate or individual plates. Mix the mustard, calamansi or lime juice, olive oil, salt and pepper and pour this dressing over the salad. Garnish with broccoli florets, fresh herbs or spring onion brushes.

Garlic can be added to the salad dressing.

CHICKEN
AND
MELON SALAD
With
WARM SESAME DRESSING

A crisp, cooling combination. Melon partners cold cooked meats very well. Arrange a bed of salad leaves on the plates first if you wish.

Serves 4-6

3 × 140 g/5 oz skinless,
   boneless chicken breasts
1 small honeydew melon
2 tbsp sesame seeds
3 tbsp sunflower oil
1 tbsp rice vinegar
2 tsp shredded ginger
2 cloves garlic, peeled and crushed
2 tsp sesame oil

Poach or steam the chicken for 8 minutes. When cool enough to handle, slice, and arrange the slices on plates, alternating with slices of melon, or put a fan of chicken slices to one side of the plate and a fan of melon slices on the other. In a small heavy fryingpan toast the sesame seeds until golden brown. Scatter them over the chicken and melon. In the same pan mix all the ingredients except the sesame oil, bring to the boil, remove from the heat, stir in the sesame oil, and spoon over the salad. Serve immediately.

CRISP CUCUMBER

Serves 4-6 as a salad, or makes a useful relish to keep in the refrigerator for adding to other dishes or serving with grilled meats. Preparation is spread over quite a time, but it is easy and can be left to drain.

> 2 cucumbers
> 1 tbsp sea salt
> 1 tbsp light muscovado sugar
> 1 tbsp rice or coconut vinegar
> 1 tsp freshly ground black pepper

Cut the ends off the cucumbers and lightly strip away about half the skin in stripes. A swivel-blade potato peeler is an excellent tool for this. Cut in half lengthways. Scoop out all the seeds. Slice the cucumber as thinly as possible and put in a wide colander. Sprinkle with salt and let the cucumber drain over a bowl for 4-6 hours. Rinse, drain and dry thoroughly between two clean teatowels. It does not matter about keeping the pieces flat. Mix the sugar, vinegar and pepper. Put the cucumber in a lidded container and stir in the dressing. Cover and refrigerate until required. The salad is unlikely to need more salt, but if it does, you can add a drop or two of soy sauce. Shredded coriander or basil leaves can be stirred in before serving. Chopped chives, spring onions or crushed garlic are other good additions, or fine rings of green or red chilli for the brave.

DIPPING SAUCE

Makes about 140 ml/5 fl oz

> 4 cloves garlic, peeled and crushed
> 1 thumb-sized piece ginger, peeled and grated
> 1 tsp soft brown sugar
> 1 tsp tomato juice
> 3 shakes of Angostura bitters
> 1 tbsp brown rice vinegar
> 1 tbsp white rice vinegar
> 3 tbsp soy sauce
> 1 tbsp toasted sesame oil
> 2 tbsp sunflower oil
> 1 tsp hot chilli oil

Mix all the ingredients thoroughly and allow to stand for an hour before using to let the flavours develop. If you mix the ingredients in a mortar with a pestle and add them in the order suggested, working in the oil last, you will get a thicker, mayonnaise-style liaison which is good for brushing on meat or fish before grilling it.

NOODLE SALADS

Chilled noodle salads are marvellous dishes, good for anytime. I sometimes serve them as a starter or as a summer lunch main course. They can also be heated up by stir-frying in the wok if you feel like a hot snack.

Transparent (mung bean) noodles, thick or thin rice noodles, buckwheat noodles or thin Japanese noodles can all be used. Failing all else, spaghettini or nests of capelli d'angelo (angel's hair) are quite acceptable substitutes. The transparent noodles are particularly good with fish.

Allow 60-85 g/2-3 oz noodles per person if serving as a starter, and 110-170 g/4-6 oz if as a main course.

Prepare the noodles as directed on the packet and then finish them as follows. Rinse the noodles thoroughly then place in a large bowl covered with cold water with half a dozen ice cubes and refrigerate until required.

Main ingredients for the salad might be fish, shellfish or chicken, all of which go well with noodles. While the main ingredient is still warm it should be mixed with a suitable dressing and some herbs and then piled on the drained chilled noodle mixture, either on individual plates or in a large bowl or shallow dish, from which everyone helps themselves.

For an informal lunch or dinner on a hot summer day make a large bowl of chilled noodles and around it arrange bowls of prepared salads, then smaller bowls of dressings, and let each guest make up their own combination. Here are a selection of salads and dressings to get you started. It is better to make separate dressings rather than cram too many flavours into one. Each salad will serve 4-6 as a starter.

Overleaf: Squid Noodle Salad with Chilli and Ginger Dressing (p. 65); plain noodles

CHICKEN NOODLE SALAD
With
PEANUT DRESSING

Serves 4-6

2 carrots
2 celery stalks
2 heaped tbsp crisp cucumber (see p. 60)
3 × 140 g/5 oz chicken breasts
3 tbsp groundnut oil
2 peeled crushed garlic cloves
15 g/½ oz coconut cream block
1-2 tbsp peanut butter
2 tsp soy sauce
1 tbsp rice vinegar
• good pinch dark muscovado sugar
• pinch ground Szechuan pepper
340 g/12 oz prepared chilled noodles
• mint leaves, optional

Peel the carrots and take off long strips with a cannelling knife or potato peeler. Trim the celery stalks and cut into very thin broad oblique slices. Mix the carrots and celery with the cucumber and put to one side. Fry the chicken breasts in the oil until cooked. Remove them, blot on kitchen paper, slice into strips and put to one side. Pour away half the oil and gently fry the garlic for a minute or two without letting it brown. Add the coconut cream and when it has melted stir in the peanut butter, soy sauce, rice vinegar, sugar and pepper. When thoroughly mixed return the chicken pieces to the pan and toss until it is well coated with the mixture. Remove the pan or wok from the heat. Drain the prepared noodles and put them in a bowl or bowls. Put the mixed vegetables on top and the chicken and dressing on top of that. Decorate with mint leaves if you wish. Serve immediately.

SHELLFISH NOODLE SALAD
With COCONUT AND
LEMON DRESSING

Serves 4-6

2-3 tbsp groundnut or grapeseed oil
8 soaked Chinese mushrooms or fresh
   shiitake mushrooms
85 g/3 oz bean sprouts
445 g/1 lb prepared shellfish,
   scallops and/or prawns
7.5 cm/3 inch piece lemon grass, sliced
85 g/3 oz coconut cream block
1 tbsp rice wine
• pinch five-spice powder
340 g/12 oz prepared
   chilled noodles
• basil leaves

Heat the oil and in it cook the mushrooms until just tender. Quickly toss in the bean sprouts and cook for a minute or two longer. Remove from the pan and put to one side. Fry the shellfish for a minute or two and remove it. Pour away half the oil and add the lemon grass, coconut cream, rice wine and spices. Mix thoroughly and remove from the heat. Drain the noodles and put them in a bowl or bowls. Arrange the vegetables on top. Quickly stir the shellfish back into the dressing and then arrange it on top of the vegetables. Decorate with shredded basil leaves.

An alternative cooking method is to steam the vegetables and the shellfish and make the dressing in a small saucepan using only a scant tablespoon of groundnut oil.

SQUID NOODLE SALAD
With CHILLI AND
GINGER DRESSING

Serves 4-6

  2 celery stalks
85 g/3 oz piece of yam bean or mooli
60 g/2 oz bean sprouts
2-3 tbsp groundnut or grapeseed oil
455 g/1 lb prepared squid
  2 tsp shredded fresh ginger
  1 small green or red chilli, seeded and
    finely sliced
  3 cloves garlic, peeled and crushed
  2 tbsp soy sauce
340 g/12 oz prepared chilled noodles
  1 red chilli "flower" for decoration

Trim the celery and slice into thin, broad, oblique pieces. Slice the yam bean or mooli similarly. Drop all three vegetables into boiling water, boil fast for a minute then drain and rinse them under cold water. Heat the oil and in it fry the squid until just cooked, opaque yet tender. With the squid still in the pan add the ginger, chilli, garlic and soy sauce. Cook for a minute more and remove the pan from the heat. Drain the chilled noodles and put them in a bowl or bowls. Arrange the vegetables on top and the seasoned squid on top of the vegetables. Decorate with the chilli to indicate that this is a spicy dish.

SALMON NOODLE SALAD
With BLACK BEAN AND
GINGER DRESSING

Serves 4-6

  1 tbsp salted black beans
85 g/3 oz bean sprouts
85 g/3 oz fresh or soaked oyster mushrooms
  2 tbsp groundnut or grapeseed oil
455 g/1 lb skinned salmon fillet cut
    into 2.5 cm/1 inch cubes,
    thoroughly dried
  2 tsp shredded fresh ginger
85 g/3 oz fresh watercress (leaves and a
    little stalk only, washed, trimmed
    and dried)
  2 tbsp rice wine, or 1 tbsp rice vinegar
    and 1-2 tbsp water
  2 tsp sesame oil
340 g/12 oz prepared, chilled noodles

Chop the black beans coarsely and steep them in 1-2 tablespoons hot water. Blanch the bean sprouts, drain and rinse them under cold water and put them to one side. Fry the mushrooms in half the oil, then remove them from the pan and put to one side. Add the rest of the oil to the pan, reheat it and fry the salmon, in batches if necessary, until just done, with a hint of gold to the flesh. Drain and put to one side. Add the ginger, the black beans and half the watercress to the pan, together with the rice wine and sesame oil. Bring to the boil for a few seconds and remove from the heat. Drain the prepared noodles and put them in a bowl or bowls. Arrange the vegetables and salmon on top. Pour the dressing on top and decorate with fresh watercress leaves.

GARLIC CHIVE PANCAKES

Another delicious way of using this exquisite herb or vegetable. Spring onions or chopped lightly fried onions can be used instead.

Makes 8-10

60 g/2 oz rice flour
40 g/1½ oz self-raising flour
● pinch of salt
2 egg whites
140 ml/7 fl oz water, or
     milk and water mixed
40 g/1½ oz finely chopped garlic chives

Sift the two flours and salt together. Beat in the egg whites and gradually add the water until you have a smooth batter of pouring consistency. Cover and let it stand for about an hour. Heat a well seasoned pan and wipe with an oiled pad of kitchen paper. When hot pour on a very thin layer of batter, swirling the pan around to get an even coating. When the top surface looks dry, turn it over with a spatula and cook the other side. Stack up the pancakes as you cook them on a plate set over hot water if serving them immediately. They can also be cooked and reheated later, over steam.

GARLIC RICE

This has become a firm favourite since we first tasted it in the Philippines. There it is very much a staple, served at most meals, and a very tasty version of fried rice. It is the traditional accompaniment to beef steak tagalog (p. 120) but I like to serve it too with grilled fish or chicken. Try it also with osso bucco or the orange and lemon braised veal shanks on p. 128. If you plan to serve it with French or Italian dishes, there is no reason why you should not substitute olive oil for the groundnut oil. If this becomes a favourite dish, it is worth preparing a larger quantity of garlic and oil and keeping it in a cool, dark place or the refrigerator.

Serves 4

    4 cloves garlic
    3 tbsp groundnut oil or sunflower oil
455 g/1 lb steamed or boiled rice

Peel and finely chop the garlic. Heat the oil in a fryingpan very gently, and add the garlic. This must not brown at all or it will take on a bitter taste and spoil the rice. The secret is to keep the heat low and be prepared to spend time letting the garlic just turn gold and translucent. Stir in the rice, and when it is well coated with oil, allow it to heat through thoroughly before spooning it into teacups, pressing it down and turning it out on to plates.

GARLIC CHIVE RISOTTO

These pungent, garlic flavoured fleshy stalks flavour a risotto perfectly. I have yet to meet anyone who does not like risotto. If you use vegetable rather than meat stock this is a lovely dish to serve to vegetarians.

Serves 6

225 g/8 oz garlic chives
 60 g/ 2 oz butter
  1 tbsp olive oil
340 g/12 oz arborio superfino rice
  • about 1.15 l/2 pints vegetable stock, kept on the boil
 85 g/3 oz freshly grated parmesan

Finely chop the garlic chives and divide into three heaps. Melt half the butter in a large frying pan and add the oil. Stir in the rice and when it is well coated with oil, add the first batch of garlic chives. Pour on 5 fl oz/140 ml stock and stir with a gentle, continuous motion until it has been absorbed. Continue adding the stock in small quantities as it is absorbed. After about 20 minutes of stirring and adding stock, the next batch of garlic chives should go in. When the rice is almost cooked and most of the liquid absorbed, the risotto should be creamy rather than dry. If not, add a little boiling water. Stir in the last batch of garlic chives and the remaining butter. Cook for 2-3 minutes more and stir in the cheese. Serve immediately.

By adding the greenery in batches you find that the first two batches impart their flavour but begin to loose colour, whilst the last batch brings a nice fresh green to the risotto.

GARLIC WILD RICE

The method used for Filipino garlic rice can be used for wild rice, using ready cooked rice, or you can do it from scratch as follows.

Serves 6

110 g/4 oz wild rice
450 ml/15 fl oz water
• pinch of salt
4 garlic cloves
4 tbsp olive oil

Put the rice, water and salt in a saucepan, bring to the boil and simmer until the rice is tender. This can take from 40-60 minutes. Peel and finely, very finely, chop the garlic and sweat it in the oil for 40-60 minutes on a very low heat. It should be translucent and almost the same colour as the oil when ready. When the rice and garlic are ready, mix the two together. Switch off the hot plate and leave to stand for a few minutes to allow the garlic flavour to permeate the hot rice. Then serve.

GARLIC CHIVE "PESTO"

This is a marvellous sauce, more like a butter really, for serving with grilled fish or steaks, and for stirring into pasta, noodles or risotto. It keeps well in the refrigerator but needs to be tightly covered as it is so very pungent. A food processor makes short work of this.

Makes about 455 g/1 lb

225 g/8 oz garlic chives
60 g/2 oz pine nuts
85 g/3 oz unsalted butter, softened
85 g/3 oz freshly grated parmesan

Finely chop the garlic chives and crush the pine nuts. Mix together thoroughly with the butter and parmesan and pack into small pots or ramekins. Cover tightly and refrigerate until required. If you cannot get pine nuts, stir in 60 g/2 oz ground almonds instead.

GARLIC CHIVE BREAD

This is well worth making your own bread dough for. Homemade bread need not be made in vast quantities, and it can be left to rise to suit you. Indeed, the dough can quite happily be left in the refrigerator to rise slowly, even overnight. I make the dough in a food processor, and 225 g/8 oz flour will make enough for four people. It is easy to double and triple the quantities. I use traditional dried active yeast, not the fast-acting variety. If you prefer the latter, then follow the method on the packet.

What makes this recipe so special, of course, is the pungent yet delicate and unusual flavour of the garlic chives. It is a lovely bread to serve with tomato soup, but is also excellent as part of an oriental-style meal. Finely chopped spring onion, or chopped and lightly fried Spanish onion can be substituted.

Makes 8–10 buns

140 ml/5 fl oz warm water
- pinch of sugar
1 tsp dried yeast
225 g/8 oz strong
plain flour ⎫ sifted together
- scant tsp salt ⎭
60 g/2 oz garlic chives including flowers,
  finely chopped

Put the water in a bowl with the sugar and sprinkle the yeast on top. After 10-15 minutes the yeasty liquid will be bubbling and rising. Pour it into the sifted flour and salt and process for 30 seconds or so. Add the garlic chives and process for another half minute or so. Remove the dough from the food processor and knead it for 10-15 minutes on a floured worktop until smooth and elastic. Work it into a ball, oil it all over and place it in an oiled bowl. Cover with cling film or a damp cloth and let it rise for 2-3 hours. Remove from the bowl. Knock back by punching all the air out of it. Break off even-sized pieces and form into buns or rolls. Brush the top and sides with oil and place on a baking tray. When doubled in volume bake in a pre-heated oven at 180°C/350°F, gas mark 4, for 15-20 minutes. Serve warm.

NOTE These buns can also be steamed and served like Cantonese *pao* or steamed bread dumplings.

CHINA

GUANGZHOU AND SHANGHAI

Travelling to Guangzhou in 1988 was at least as exciting as being there. Like the time we took the train from Venice to Zagreb a few years earlier, across February snowfields, it was travelling from the known to the unknown, crossing significant borders.

From the Peninsula Hotel's silent green Rolls Royce into the hustle and bustle of Hung Hom railway station in Kowloon was another kind of border-crossing. The station was crowded. There were queues for the Guangzhou train, in different places, for different kinds of seats. We found our way to a small waiting area where our luggage, ourselves and our visas were given a brief inspection, and we went through Immigration, down to the platform and to a most delightful train. In first class the seats had cream loose covers, antimacassars and lace curtains. By the time the train left, on time, it was full. Every so often young women in uniforms would wheel trolleys of wonderful-smelling food up and down the aisle. No plastic trays and pre-packed food here: we were offered blue and white porcelain bowls of soup, of rice and vegetables, of cooked meat. There were a few Westerners, but the passengers were mainly Chinese, families, business people, young men beautifully dressed in the height of fashion, many carrying bulging shopping bags, boxes of electrical goods and large toys.

The crowded streets and high-rise dwellings of Kowloon disappeared suddenly as we entered a tunnel and on emerging, we crossed the more open New Territories, passing smallholdings, ponds, farms, and quiet villages until we reached Lo Wu, the border crossing. The train stopped on both sides but little fuss was made. No-one seemed to get on or off. We travelled on into Shenzhen, one of the booming special economic zones of the People's Republic. Truth to tell it looked very like Kowloon, with its new buildings, garish signs, and conspicuous consumerism. The clue that we had crossed a border was the number of bicycles, far more than we had seen in Kowloon.

After that it was a pleasant ride through the fertile South China plain. It was February, just before Chinese New Year, and the countryside, although rich green and intensively farmed, was rather featureless. Small images remain: white ducks on ponds;

farmers in conical hats cycling along levees; water buffalo pulling ploughs across rich brown earth. It was rural indeed.

The signs of industry came soon enough as we began to slow down on entry to Guangzhou. As the train reaches the city centre it runs parallel to the Huanshi Road, one of the city's main east-west thoroughfares. The railway station is to the north of the city, the Pearl River to the south. Between the two are most of the city sights: Yuexiu Park, the Orchid Garden, the Dr Sun Yat Sen Memorial Hall, the Guangxiao Temple between Dongfeng Road West and Zongshan Road 7, the beautiful Flowery Pagoda in the grounds of the Liurong Temple, the mosque and minaret in Guangta Road, and Shamian Island on the Pearl River. It is on Shamian Island, which was once out of bounds to the Chinese after sunset, that you will find the famous White Swan Hotel, all polished red granite, fountains and extraordinary ornamental trees made of polished quartz and jade. A vast hotel with views of the Pearl River, this would be well worth staying in for a night or two. More parks, gardens and hotels lie to the east of the city, which is where we stayed at the Garden Hotel. This would be an imposing building anywhere, but here, in contrast to its drab surroundings, it is breathtaking. The vast reception hall is decorated with a most extraordinary mural in gold on black marble, depicting traditional Chinese figures, landscapes and emblems. We did not see anything quite as grand during our stay in Guangzhou.

It was the famous "Canton market" that had brought us here. Many people in Hong Kong counselled against it, saying that we would find it cruel and objectionable to see live animals and birds in cages being sold for food. Neither of us was feeling particularly robust and stony-hearted on the morning we visited it. Set back off Chingping Road, the market runs along two streets forming a cross, each "arm" of which concentrates on a particular type of produce. The fruit and vegetable "arms" were interesting enough, well-stocked with handsome tropical fruits and leafy greens. But we were interested to see the meat sections. There were butchers' stalls selling different cuts of raw meat, some of it recognizably dog. And the livestock cages did hold cats, frogs, rats, puppies and other small animals. But it was not gruesome or cruel. I have seen far more cruel sights in pet shops in Britain. And who can call the Guangzhou market cruel and inhumane and yet eat pork and chicken raised in our intensive animal farming systems in Britain?

The most fascinating part of the market was, as so often, the dry goods and medicine section. I have great admiration for a culture that does not separate healing from nourishing, which in order to preserve the body's Yin and Yang prescribes different kinds of foods rather than pills and potions. Thus the exquisite and expensive flower mushrooms are more often to be found in a Chinese pharmacy or on a herbalist's stall than in a food shop. They were just as expensive here in Guangzhou as they were in Taipei and Hong Kong. We bought inexpensive ginseng, young roots, so that I would be able to make ginseng chicken on cold November days in London.

Although Guangzhou and the region is the original home of the finest of Chinese cuisines, it was not Cantonese cooking that made our visit so memorable. Back at the Garden Hotel, General Manager Herbert Sossner and his English chef Neil had planned a most extraordinary dinner for us. We started with caviar of very fine quality, large-grained and brownish grey. Fresh foie gras, just a slice, pan-fried and served on crunchy celeriac followed, and that in turn was followed by a tender, cushiony fillet of veal with a sauce of mixed mushrooms. Pudding was three kinds of strawberries. Nothing very surprising, you might think, for a luxury five-star hotel with an international clientele, used to having first-class produce flown in from all over the world. But it was surprising, for everything we ate that evening was locally produced, in and around Guangzhou. The caviar was mandarin, not beluga, and it is very good indeed. Sometimes, I am told, it can be a little salty. Apparently the trick is to pour it into a fine nylon mesh sieve and pour a small bottle of Tsingtao beer over it. This is also a very useful trick to use to improve the flavour of other, lesser sorts of fish roe such as salmon or trout eggs that have been preserved with too much salt.

The main purpose of our visit to Shanghai, our next port-of-call, was not to sample the food but to spend a Saturday evening at the Peace Hotel, listening to their legendary jazz band. The Peace Hotel is the former Cathay Hotel, scene of Vicki Baum's *Shanghai '37* and J. G. Ballard's *Empire of the Sun.* It was an unforgettable evening. We went first to see the Shanghai acrobats at their theatre, which is almost like a fixed Big Top in the Nanjing Road. We had the best two seats in the house, in the front row opposite the acrobats' entrance to the ring. They were such fun: agile, skilled, handsome to watch, breathtaking and literally death-defying in some of their tricks.

At about 9.30 we walked into the perfect thirties interior of the Peace Hotel. Cool jazz drew us towards the Coffee Shop, and miraculously we found a table at the front. There were octagonal tables, covered with white cloths topped with glass, and solid-backed chairs of light wood which matched the panelling on the walls and the columns. Dim wall lights were enhanced that evening by television lights. It is said that the jazz band here has been filmed by every television company in the world. They were brilliant and easily worth the journey to Shanghai. Five men in their sixties and seventies, a pianist, a drummer, a double bass player and two saxophonists, dressed in black western-style suits with white shirts and ties, played the sweetest music imaginable, including much Glenn Miller, in a lively smoky atmosphere. We drank cans of Tsingtao beer.

Later in the evening, as it got noisier and smokier, couples danced, men and women, and women together. The faces of the local people showed a fascinating blend of cosmopolitan character-istics, such as you are likely to find only in one of the world's major port cities. A group of very expensively dressed yet curiously old-fashioned young men came in with their glamorous and highly made-up female companions. They looked like the underworld of Shanghai and were given the best table and the most exotic-looking drinks. The dark green coated, bow-tied waiters were smooth and efficient and we felt as if we were in a forties film directed by Marcel Carné.

On another occasion we lunched at the Peace Hotel in the top floor Chinese restaurant overlooking the Bund, where we were served two Shanghai specialities, eels in a hot stewy sauce, and a bowl of efu noodles. Mr Wang Shiting, the General Manager, joined us for tea afterwards and told us of the hotel's plans for renovation and refurbishment in keeping with the original design. We loved Shanghai. We enjoyed walking along the Bund and never tired of simply standing, leaning on the parapet and watching the life of the busy river. Clearly it was a favourite local pastime too since the parapet was always crowded with river gazers.

The street markets in Shanghai were definitely not on the tourist trail. We were stared at with much more open curiosity here than in Guangzhou. February can be a bitterly cold month in

Shanghai but with the clear skies and weak sun, it felt almost springlike. In some of the markets, bundles of pussy willow and catkins were for sale, alongside the mountains of cabbages, rows of gleaming fresh fish and sacks of rice, corn and pulses. Two images are clearly etched in my mind. One is of a young woman, warmly wrapped and wearing stout boots and fingerless mittens, standing at a stall behind a bucket of eels, each one about three inches long, a silvery writhing mass. She would take one out of the bucket with her left hand and with a swift, almost invisible motion of her right thumb would split and bone the eel in a flash, adding it to the growing heap of prepared eels. At another stall, this one more sheltered and warmed anyway by the steaming cauldron, a friendly faced woman wearing a white cap and overall with blue sleeve protectors was rolling out dough, cutting circles, filling and pinching them together to make plump little wontons. I was fascinated by the manual dexterity of both these women.

The Jade Buddha Temple on Anyuan Lu is not much more than a hundred years old, but it has the feeling of being ageless. Inside, it is quiet but not hushed. Monks and visitors go about their business. Some come to pray, to leave offerings or to have their fortune told. Some come simply to look. There are fine strangely terrifying statues of the Iron Goddess of Mercy and two beautifully tranquil white jade buddhas, brought to Shanghai from Burma by the monk Huigen. Within the temple is a simple restaurant, serving Buddhist vegetarian food. It smelled very good.

Not far away is the Yuyuan Market and Yuyuan Garden, in which it is easy to wander away a morning or afternoon, perhaps having lunch in one of the many restaurants in this old section of the city. It is an area of small, criss-crossing streets, of dwellings and shops selling food, clothes, crafts and all kinds of other merchandise. We even passed the Shanghai Snuff Shop. Within this same area is a lake with a tea house on an island which is reached by a strange zigzagging bridge. The angles and corners prevent evil spirits from following you across the bridge. The Yuyuan Garden is a pleasant walled landscaped garden surrounding a mansion built in the Ming dynasty. Pavilions, towers, terraces and delicate bridges make this an attractive, peaceful place to visit if the noise and bustle of the city becomes too much. Shanghai is indeed a noisy, crowded city, vying with Tokyo, Mexico City and Sao Paulo as the world's largest. Though it has relatively few cars, there are still traffic jams, because of buses, bicycles, lorries, one-way streets and failed traffic lights. Busy road junctions do not have pedestrian crossings, but pedestrian bridges, high above the traffic. Yet there are pockets of the city that are calm and quiet. On the way into the city from the airport one drives along wide pleasant, tree-lined boulevards, glimpsing imposing Edwardian-style and mock Tudor mansions behind high walls and yew hedges. It might be Weybridge. This was part of the international concession, where the large settlements of British and French lived. Again, we felt as though we were in a film, only this time it was Spielberg's *Empire of the Sun*.

Even in those early days of its opening the Shanghai Hilton was the place to eat. Its General Manager, Heinz Schwander, had been trained as a chef and he was still a dedicated cook. His enthusiasm was great as he described the new restaurants to us; a Hunanese restaurant with a chef and his whole brigade being brought in, the Shanghai Express which would serve inexpensive local food, the Teppan Grill which was to be an innovative mixture of Japanese and classical French, and the Sui Yuan, the Cantonese restaurant where we had a very fine meal. Chef Lo from Hong Kong invented a salad for us of chicken with hami melon and sesame seeds. It was, he said, based on two or three "classical" Cantonese recipes, and provided the inspiration for my chicken salad on p. 59. My recipe for almond beancurd on p. 158 is not far removed from the one Chef Lo prepared for us, but his, with its splash of crème de menthe, was even more of an East-West mélange. Chef Lo has worked in Canada and South America as well as China and Hong Kong and he readily admitted to using and developing ideas he had collected in his travels, hence the bottle of crème de menthe that he kept in his kitchen.

He could not have been in better company. The executive chef was Peter Knipp, who had come there via Singapore. He was already very well known and had won awards for his skilful blending of eastern and western cooking, particularly his use of oriental ingredients and European techniques. We had long discussions about the validity and integrity of this kind of cooking and Peter Knipp helped me reaffirm my view that there is every justification for welcoming into one's kitchen a whole new range of flavours and textures. I am grateful for the advice and encouragement he gave me.

FISH

FISH STOCK

Since a number of the recipes call for fish stock, here is my standard and very adaptable recipe, as a base for sauces or soups. When you buy fish, sole for example, ask your fishmonger to fillet it and wrap the bones, head and skin separately, together with any other bones that can be spared. I do not like the flavour given by prawn shells and trimmings and would not normally use them, but lobster shells are another matter.

Whenever possible, try to make your stock well in advance and with plenty of ventilation. Regrettably the smell of fish stock does linger everywhere.

Makes about 1 litre/1¾ pints

- 1 tsp groundnut or sunflower oil
- 1 onion
- 1 carrot
- 1 celery stick
- 1 leek
- watercress, parsley, fennel etc. – whatever you have available
- 1-2 squashy tomatoes
- 680 g/1½ lb fish bones and pieces, chopped to fit your saucepan
- 1 litre/1¾ pints water

Use the oil simply to rub around a heavy saucepan to stop bits sticking to it. Peel and chop or slice the vegetables and turn these in the pan until *just* beginning to turn colour. Add the fish bones and pieces and cook until opaque. Pour on the water and bring slowly to the boil. Simmer gently, covered, for 40 minutes. Strain. Cool and refrigerate until required. Do not season since the stock will often need to be much reduced for a sauce, and salting at the stock-making stage will ruin the end result.

GINGER SALMON FILLETS
With
ALMOND BUTTER

I would not, I think, recommend this treatment for wild salmon, which is best cooked and served as simply as possible, but for farmed salmon, pink trout, rainbow trout, and indeed any firm oily fish which can take a spicy marinade, this is a delicious recipe. The skin keeps the flesh moist as it cooks and looks good when you serve it, a lovely golden brown. This is also a good method for cooking small pieces of fish that you want to serve cold. When the fish is cooked, transfer it to a plate, or foil covered tray, skin side up. The juices are kept in on both sides, and you remove the skin just before serving. Obviously a melting butter sauce is not the thing to serve with a piece of cold salmon. How about a ginger-flavoured mayonnaise?

Serves 4

- 4 salmon fillets weighing about 170 g/6 oz, and roughly the same size and shape
- 1 onion
- 5 cm/2 inches smooth, fresh ginger (not an old wrinkly knob)
- 6 tbsp dry white vermouth, such as Noilly Prat
- • freshly ground white pepper
- 30 g/1 oz chilled unsalted butter
- 30 g/1 oz blanched crushed almonds

Remove any bones from the fish and trim the fillets if necessary to make nice neat shapes. Peel and slice the onion thinly. Place the onion rings in a single layer over the bottom of a shallow dish. Peel the ginger and shave off several slices with a potato peeler. Lay these over the onions. Sprinkle on the vermouth and white pepper. Place the fillets of salmon on top, skin side up, and press them down so that the whole fillet comes into contact with some onion and ginger. Leave for 20 minutes.

Meanwhile, cover the grill rack with foil, turning up the edges to catch any cooking juices. Lightly oil or butter the foil and put the grill on at full heat. Remove the salmon from the marinade, picking off any pieces of onion and ginger, and pat it dry with kitchen paper. Place the fillets on the grill rack skin side up and grill for 2 minutes with the grill full on. Turn down to moderate heat and grill for a further 3-4 minutes, depending on the thickness of the fish and how well done you like it.

Remove the fish and keep it warm. Strain the cooking juices and the marinade into a small fryingpan or saucepan. Boil until syrupy, stir in the chilled butter, a small piece at a time, until the sauce thickens, stir in the almonds, and then pour on to four heated dinner plates. Place the fish on the plates, garnish if you wish, and serve.

Overleaf: Dominoes of Salmon in Soy and Tomato Butter (p. 81); Vegetable "Noodles" (p. 154)

MARINATED GRILLED FISH

If serving as part of an oriental meal, one or two fish will suffice. This is a particularly suitable method for cooking flat fish. Indeed, I first tried it out on dabs, which were quite transformed by the aromatic flavours of ginger and sesame oil. You can use the same initial preparation for small whole round fish, such as trout, grey mullet or mackerel, but it is then better steamed than grilled because the cooking is more even.

Serves 4

4   dabs or other flat fish, scaled and
      weighing about 340 g/12 oz each
2.5 cm/1 inch chunk peeled
      fresh ginger root
4   large garlic cloves
4   tbsp soy sauce
4   tbsp grapeseed or groundnut oil
1   tbsp light sesame oil
1   tbsp rice wine
4   spring onions, finely sliced

With a sharp knife, make 5 or 6 shallow diagonal slashes, herring-bone fashion, on either side of the backbone, both sides of the fish. Cut the ginger root and garlic into fine slivers and put them in a small saucepan together with the soy sauce, oils and rice wine. Bring to simmering point, lay the fish on a large flat dish and pour the marinade over them, spooning it into the slashes on the fish. Turn after 30 minutes or so to make sure that the fish absorb as much flavour as possible and leave for up to an hour in a cool place.

Heat the grill, and when very hot, place the fish on it pale skin down. Grill for 3 minutes but not much more, then carefully turn the fish and grill on the other side for 1 or 2 minutes. If the fish is very thin and the grill was very hot when you started cooking, the fish might not need turning.

Transfer the fish to heated dinner plates. Heat up any remaining marinade, pour over the fish and scatter the spring onions on top.

COOL AND HOT PRAWNS

Despite the lengthy list of ingredients this is a very simple dish to prepare. It makes an excellent starter served on individual plates or can be passed round as something to accompany pre-dinner drinks. The sauces can also be served with crudités, small skewers of grilled meats or fish or deep-fried prawns.

Serves 6-8

1.1 kg/2½ lb prawns in the shell
1   tsp fine sea salt
570 ml/1 pint Evian or
      other still bottled water

COOL SAUCE

1   tbsp chopped fresh mint,
      or ½ tbsp dried mint
½ cucumber
2   tsp sea salt
1   tbsp fresh coriander leaves
60 g/2 oz dill pickle or gherkins,
      chopped or sliced
3   tbsp thick yogurt
● freshly ground white pepper

HOT SAUCE

2 cloves garlic
4 spring onions, or 2 shallots
  or small onions
1 small sweet red pepper ⎫
1 tiny hot red pepper   ⎪ seeds and pith
1 small sweet green pepper ⎬ removed
1 tiny hot green pepper ⎭
2 fresh ripe tomatoes,
  peeled and seeded
1 tbsp toasted sesame oil
3 tbsp groundnut oil
1 tbsp soy sauce
2 tsp rice vinegar

Peel the prawns and tie the shells in a piece of damp muslin. Put the prawns, salt and shells in a bowl. Cover with water and chill for an hour or so until required, but do not let them stand for much more than 2 hours.

To make the cool sauce, put the mint in a bowl and pour on 4 tablespoons boiling water. Cut the cucumber in half lengthways and scoop out the seeds. Chop or roughly slice, put in a colander and sprinkle with salt. Let it drain for about an hour, then rinse and dry thoroughly. Put the mint and its liquid, the coriander, cucumber, pickle and yogurt in a blender or food processor and blend until smooth. Season to taste. Spoon into a bowl and chill until required.

For the hot sauce peel and chop the garlic and onions and put them together with the rest of the ingredients in a blender or food processor and blend until smooth. Season to taste, spoon into a bowl and chill until required.

To serve, drain the prawns and arrange them on two plates around the bowls of sauce.

DOMINOES OF SALMON IN SOY AND TOMATO BUTTER

Serves 4

680 g/1½ lb salmon fillet
• white pepper
110 g/4 oz shallots
60 g/2 oz unsalted butter
300 ml/10 fl oz fish stock
85 g/3 oz peeled, seeded
  and diced tomatoes
4 tbsp soy sauce

Skin the salmon fillet, flatten it slightly and remove the bones. Trim off the ragged edges and the pointed tail end. Cut across the fillet into 2.5 cm/1 inch wide strips, season the fish lightly with pepper and put to one side while you start the sauce.

Peel and finely chop the shallots and fry them gently in half the butter. Cook until soft and almost melted. Add the fish stock and let this simmer until reduced by half. Meanwhile, heat a non-stick fryingpan and cook the pieces of salmon very quickly, for about half a minute on each side. Remove from the pan and keep the fish warm. Continue cooking the sauce, now over a high heat, adding any salmon juices from the non-stick pan. Add the tomato and pour in the soy sauce, bubble until reduced a little further and add the rest of the butter piece by piece, swirling and shaking the pan back and forth to amalgamate with the sauce.

Divide the sauce among four heated dinner plates and lay the salmon dominoes on top, overlapping. Serve with new potatoes, rice or homemade wholewheat pasta and a green vegetable or salad.

BRAISED GREY MULLET

Use a fish kettle or a large roasting tin.

Serves 4

900 g/2 lb grey mullet
75 ml/3 fl oz groundnut oil
2 tbsp finely chopped parsley
2 tbsp chopped coriander
2 cloves garlic, peeled and crushed
1 piece lemon grass
1 piece orange peel
6 ripe tomatoes, peeled,
   seeded and diced
4 tbsp rice wine
4 tbsp fish stock
6 slices fresh ginger
1 tbsp fermented black beans

Have your fishmonger scale, gut and clean the mullet. Gently heat the oil in the roasting tin or fish kettle and when it is hot, add the parsley, coriander, garlic, lemon grass and orange peel. Lower the heat and lay the fish on top. Cook gently for 5 minutes then add the tomatoes, rice wine, fish stock, ginger and black beans. Cover and cook for a further 10-15 minutes, depending on the thickness of the fish. Gently lift it on to a serving dish and pour the cooking juices over it. Serve hot with steamed or boiled rice or noodles, spring onions and slices of lemon or lime. It is also very good served with steamed or boiled potatoes.

Previous page: Fish Baked in a Bag with Fennel, Kumquat and Ginger Butter

FRIED SQUID With STEAMED VEGETABLE RIBBONS

A swivel-head potato peeler is invaluable here for shaving the vegetables into ribbons. When I first tasted this dish, Bettina, my sister-in-law, had prepared it with crisp broccoli florets. I like the colourful mix of vegetables which look like a pile of noodles.

Serves 4

SQUID

4 medium-size squid,
   about 15-20 cm/
   6-8 inches long
1 tbsp groundnut oil
1 shallot, finely chopped
1 tsp grated fresh ginger root
1 tbsp concentrated fish stock or
   oyster sauce

VEGETABLES

1 mooli or white radish,
   about 15 cm/6 inches
2 long straight carrots
1 parsnip, if available
110 g/4 oz celeriac root, if available
2 sticks celery
2 leeks
● seasoning

Clean and empty the squid. Peel off the outer skin, open out and cut it down the middle. Lightly score the fish with a sharp knife point in straight lines about 5 mm/¼ inch apart. Score across these with the knife blade held at an oblique angle. Then cut into triangular pieces.

   Peel and trim the vegetables. Shave the root

vegetables into 5 mm/¼ inch wide ribbons. Slice the celery into long thin strips. Quarter the leeks lengthways and separate into ribbons. Cut the wider ones into two. Lightly season the vegetables and pile into a steamer basket. Set over boiling water and steam for no more than 5 minutes.

Heat the groundnut oil in a wok or fryingpan and quickly fry the squid with the shallot and ginger. After a couple of minutes, add the fish stock or sauce. Stir briskly for another minute over a high heat and serve immediately with the vegetable ribbons.

FISH BAKED IN A BAG
With
FENNEL, KUMQUAT AND GINGER BUTTER

The recipe I give here is for a whole fish, such as a sea bass, grey mullet or salmon. It can be used for smaller fish such as red mullet or rainbow trout to make individual portions. Have your fishmonger gut and, if necessary, scale the fish, removing the eyes but leaving the head on.

Serves 4-6

1 fish weighing about 1 kg/2¼ lb
85 g/3 oz softened butter
110 g/4 oz Florentine fennel
85 g/3 oz kumquats
1 piece crystallized ginger
½ tsp sea salt
- *pinch of white pepper*

Make the butter in a food processor if possible. Put the softened butter into the bowl of the food processor. Roughly chop the fennel and add to the butter. Cut the kumquats in half and remove the seeds. Squeeze the juice into the butter, remove the centre of the kumquat and place the skins in the food processor together with the ginger. Add a little salt and pepper. Process until smooth and well blended.

Take a sheet of foil or heavy duty greaseproof paper large enough to wrap the fish entirely. Smear some of the butter mixture on the foil and lay the fish on top. Place half the remaining mixture inside the fish and spread the rest on top. Wrap the foil or paper round the fish and close tightly. Place the parcel on a baking sheet, place in a preheated oven, 180°C/350°F, gas mark 4, and bake for 25-30 minutes.

Remove the parcel carefully, open one end of it and let the juices run into a jug to serve as a sauce with the fish. If you wish you can boil the juice up with a tablespoon of cream and a little white wine to make a richer sauce.

SALMON WONTONS

These make an excellent starter, or serve them as snacks with drinks. If you have salmon or other fish stock you can serve the dumplings in it as a soup course.

Makes 24

170-225 g/6-8 oz raw salmon
   3 spring onions
   2 cm/1 ½ inch chunk fresh ginger
   2 cloves garlic
  60 g/2 oz fresh bean sprouts
   2 tbsp soy sauce
   2 tsp light sesame oil
   2 tsp rice vinegar
   1 tsp fish or oyster sauce
 24 fresh wonton wrappers
    (from Chinese supermarkets)
140 ml/5 fl oz fish stock

GARNISH

- fresh coriander leaves, chives or garlic chives

Skin the salmon, remove the bones and chop into very fine dice. I would hesitate to use a food processor as there is a danger of processing the fish too long, resulting in a paste.

Peel and finely chop the spring onions, ginger and garlic and mix with the salmon. Wash the bean sprouts, roughly chop them and then add to the fish. Moisten the mixture with half the soy sauce, sesame oil, rice vinegar and fish or oyster sauce. Take one wonton wrapper and moisten it with water to help it seal, place a small teaspoon of the salmon mixture in the centre and bring the corners and centre to the middle, pinching together to seal. Fill the rest of the wontons in the same way. Lightly oil a steamer tray or basket and steam the wontons for 8 minutes.

Meanwhile, make the sauce by boiling up the stock with the rest of the soy sauce, sesame oil, vinegar and fish or oyster sauce. Pour into a bowl and serve with the wontons. Garnish with the greenery.

SKATE With SESAME OIL

Skate is one of the few fish which, like Dover sole, improves with keeping an extra day or so. If cooked when too fresh it is bland and tasteless, though we are less likely nowadays to be able to buy it "too fresh". An alternative to the traditional skate with black butter is to steam it and then serve it with a sprinkling of sesame oil and soy sauce.

Serves 4

900 g-1.1 kg/2-2½lb skate wings,
   in 4 pieces
- salt, pepper
1 tbsp tamarind water or
   lemon juice
- coriander leaves or
   garlic chives to garnish
2 tbsp sesame oil
1 tbsp soy sauce

Wipe the fish with kitchen paper. Season it lightly and rub with tamarind or lemon juice. Arrange in a lightly oiled steamer basket or on a plate to fit over a pan of simmering water. Cover and steam gently for 10-12 minutes. Arrange on heated dinner plates, garnish with coriander or garlic chives. Heat the sesame oil and soy sauce and pour it over the fish at the table.

SALMON STEAKS STUFFED
With
GARLIC CHIVES AND LEMON GRASS SAUCE

This is a rich dish for special occasions, not for everyday dining.

Serves 4

4 × 4 cm/1 ½ inch salmon steaks
1 bunch of garlic chives weighing
  about 225 g/8 oz
3 shallots
60 g/2 oz unsalted butter
300 ml/10 fl oz fish stock
1 piece of lemon grass
140 ml/7 fl oz dry white wine
3 tbsp double cream
● seasoning

Trim the garlic chives of any wilted or discoloured parts. Reserve some flowering tips for garnish. Chop the stalks quite small. Peel and chop the shallots and cook the two vegetables in half the unsalted butter in a small saucepan until soft. Put into a blender and process until smooth.

Simmer the fish stock, lemon grass and white wine for 15 minutes. Strain into another saucepan. Boil the liquid until reduced by at least two thirds.

Butter an ovenproof dish and lay the salmon steaks in it. Season them lightly and cover with buttered paper. Bake for 8 minutes in a preheated oven, 180°C/350°F, gas mark 4. Remove from the oven and carefully take out the central bone. Fill the cavity with the garlic chive mixture. Pour the cream into the reduced stock and bubble until syrupy. Spoon this over the salmon steaks and pass quickly under a hot grill to lightly brown the top.

SCRAMBLED EGGS AND OYSTERS

This is based on a delicious Chiu Chow recipe from the southwestern part of China. It is very quick to cook and makes an excellent lunch or supper dish. Thawed frozen oysters can be used, or fresh mussels, but oysters really are better.

Serves 4

6 eggs
1 tbsp melted butter
1 tbsp soy sauce
1-2 tbsp chopped spring onions
  or garlic chives
1 tbsp groundnut oil
12-16 shucked oysters

Beat the eggs, butter and soy sauce. Stir in the greens. Heat the oil in a frying pan and put in the oysters. Pour on the eggs immediately and cook gently until done. In Chinese restaurants I have eaten a version that is halfway between scrambled eggs and an omelette, with the eggs turned over and cooked to a golden brown on the other side. Both versions are good.

SHRIMP-STUFFED MUSHROOMS

This mixture can also be used to stuff parboiled courgettes or small hollowed-out potatoes, which have been cooked until just tender. A mixture of shiitake, oyster and ordinary cap mushrooms would be delicious if you can't get dried flower mushrooms. If you do use the latter, they should be soaked for 30 minutes, rinsed and then simmered for 15 minutes in stock, wine or water. Only raw prawns should be used. These are usually sold frozen.

Serves 4-6

As a starter

18 mushrooms about
   4 cm/1½ inches in diameter
2 tsp cornflour
455 g/1 lb raw prawns, shelled
1 egg white
- large pinch salt
- small pinch pepper
- finely grated ginger and chopped chive or spring onion for garnish

Remove the stalks from the mushrooms and wipe them clean. Avoid washing them if possible. Sprinkle cornflour lightly over the inside of each mushroom cap, which helps stick the stuffing to it. Put the shelled prawns, most of the egg white, the remaining cornflour, the salt and pepper in a food processor and process, or chop with two heavy cleavers, until you have a smooth paste. Spoon the filling into each mushroom cap and smooth it over with a finger or thumb dipped into the egg white. Place in a steamer basket and steam for 8 minutes. Remove and garnish before serving.

MACKEREL With FIVE-SPICE, MUSTARD AND CORIANDER

Cooking fish in a roasting bag removes the need for even the slightest trace of oil or butter and leaves you with no pots and pans to wash. I also like the very fresh-tasting dishes produced by this method.

Serves 4

4 mackerel, about 280 g/10 oz each
2 tbsp mustard
4 tbsp finely chopped coriander
   (parsley or watercress
   can substitute)
1 tsp five-spice powder
2 crushed garlic cloves, optional
- seasoning
2 tbsp wholemeal breadcrumbs

The mackerel should be gutted and cleaned, heads on or off according to your preference. Slash each side diagonally in 3 places. Mix the mustard, coriander, spice powder, garlic and seasoning and spoon it into the slashes. Press the breadcrumbs into the surface. Use 2 roasting bags and place 2 fish in each, tightly closing the bag but cutting a slit in each to let the steam escape. Bake in a medium oven, 180°C/350°F, gas mark 4, for 25 minutes.

STEAMED SCALLOP DINNER

With an electric steamer, a set of bamboo baskets placed in a wok or a three-tiered steamer which fits on top of the stove, you can cook a whole meal in one go. You could even use a camping stove with a single burner if you used parboiled rice. Put the rice in the first tier as it takes longer to cook, then add the basket of vegetables and finally the scallops. Use diagonally sliced carrots and celery, broccoli florets, green beans, beansprouts, mangetouts, white radish.

Serves 4

6 tbsp rice vinegar
4 star anise pods
1 piece tangerine or orange peel
2.5 cm/1 inch piece fresh ginger, peeled and shredded, or sliced and cut into slivers
170 g/6 oz rice
½ tsp salt
340 g/12 oz prepared vegetables
8-12 scallops
3 cloves garlic, peeled, sliced and cut into slivers
2 tsp fermented black beans
4 spring onions, shredded
2-3 tbsp soy sauce
1 tsp chilli oil

Mix half the rice vinegar with 570 ml/1 pint water, add 2 star anise pods, the dried peel and ginger peelings and place in the pan or wok which is going to be the base of the steamer.

In another pan bring the rice to the boil in twice its volume of water with the salt. Simmer with the lid on for 10 minutes. Drain, rinse and drain again and place it in a steamer basket, lined with muslin if it has large holes. Steam the rice for 5 minutes and while it is steaming, prepare the vegetables and place them in the second steamer basket which you fit on top of the rice.

Steam the vegetables for 5-8 minutes while you prepare the scallops. Remove the pieces of tough muscle from the scallops and any skin and dirt. Pat dry in paper towels. Put the scallops in the third steamer basket. On top of the scallops scatter the thinnest slivers of garlic and fresh ginger, with the black beans, spring onions and remaining star anise pods. Sprinkle on a few drops of soy sauce. Place the third steamer basket over the vegetables, cover with a lid and steam for 3 minutes only. This is sufficient to cook the scallops.

If you are using bamboo baskets, these can be brought to the table and everyone can help themselves using chopsticks and bowls. A dipping sauce can be made by adding a little chilli oil to the remaining soy sauce and rice vinegar.

Overleaf: Steamed Scallop Dinner

SOUSED ORIENTAL SALMON

This recipe is based on an old-fashioned preparation, originally for herrings when they used to be cheap and plentiful. I have adapted it to oriental ingredients.

Serves 8

As a starter

MARINADE

570 ml/1 pint brown rice vinegar
570 ml/1 pint rice wine
12 star anise pods
6 cloves
3 bay leaves
3 kaffir lime leaves
• seeds from 6 cardamom pods
12 black peppercorns
1 tbsp sea salt
2 tbsp unrefined sugar
1 small salmon – 900 g-1.35kg/2-3 lb, cleaned and gutted with head and backbone removed (keep for stock)
1 tbsp Chinese mustard
2 large mild onions
3 tbsp capers

Put the marinade ingredients in a saucepan, bring to the boil, simmer for 10-15 minutes and allow to cool. Open the salmon out flat, wipe it and remove as many bones as you can, as well as any hard or finny bits. Spread it with mustard. Peel and thinly slice the onions and lay the smaller onion rings over the fish. Sprinkle the capers on top. Roll the salmon from tail to shoulder and secure it with toothpicks. Place the rolled salmon in a lightly oiled, deep ovenproof dish and pour over the strained marinade. Cover the dish with a lid or foil and bake for 30 minutes in the centre of a preheated oven, 180°C/350°F, gas mark 4. Leave the salmon to cool in the marinade and then refrigerate for two days.

Slice and serve with brown bread and butter.

STEAMED CLAMS
AND
FENNEL

Match the fennel with a few star anise pods to flavour the steam. It makes a delicious starter served in soup bowls, or part of a main course if served with rice or noodles.

Serves 4-6

3 star anise
1 fennel bulb
900 g/2 lb Venus clams
• white pepper

Place the star anise in a saucepan of water or in the bottom of an electric steamer with the correct amount of water and bring to the boil. Trim any discoloured parts from the fennel, cut into quarters and finely slice each piece. Put it straight into a steamer basket, cover and steam for 4-5 minutes. Rinse the clams thoroughly, place them on top of the fennel and steam until they open. Season with white pepper, scatter on any feathery fennel leaves and serve immediately.

COD *With a* BLACK BEAN, PEANUT *AND* GINGER CRUST

Serves 4

4 × 170 g/6 oz thick cod fillets, skins
    removed
- salt and pepper
30 g/1 oz dry roasted unsalted
    peanuts, crushed
30 g/1 oz fermented black beans
1 tsp freshly grated ginger
85 g/3 oz fresh white breadcrumbs
580 ml/1 pint fish stock
1 lemon grass stalk, thinly sliced
3 tbsp dry vermouth
110 g/4 oz unsalted butter, 30g/1 oz of it
    softened and 30 g/1 oz chilled and diced
2 tbsp double cream

Remove any bones from the fish, lightly season
on both sides. Cover and refrigerate until
required while you prepare the topping and the
sauce. Mix the peanuts, black beans, ginger and
breadcrumbs. Simmer the stock, lemon grass
and vermouth and allow to reduce by half. Strain
into a clean saucepan.

Melt 60 g/2 oz butter in a fryingpan and
gently cook the fish until just firm. Carefully
remove from the pan and transfer to a buttered
baking sheet. Brush the top surface of the fillets
with softened butter and press in the crumble
topping. Place under a hot grill to brown it.
Meanwhile, finish the sauce by pouring in any
cooking juices and reducing further. Whisk in
the diced butter, and when fully incorporated
stir in the cream, season to taste and spoon on to
heated dinner plates. Arrange the fish fillets on
top and garnish with lemon verbena leaves.

STEAMED FISH

This is the method I have seen used by
many Chinese cooks and it can hardly
be improved upon. You can, of course,
change the flavourings, perhaps adding some
coriander leaves, star anise, or dried tangerine peel. At a Cantonese banquet the fish
will usually be a firm sweet-fleshed grouper.
A small cod, a grilse (small salmon), salmon
trout, sea bass or grey mullet can be cooked
in the same way.

Serves 4-6

1.1-1.35 kg/2½-3 lb round fish, gutted but
    left whole with the head intact
1 bunch spring onions or baby leeks
5 cm/2 inch piece fresh ginger
2-3 cloves of garlic
4 tbsp soy sauce
2 tbsp good dry sherry or rice wine
1 tbsp toasted sesame oil

Rinse and dry the fish thoroughly. Wash the
spring onions or baby leeks, cut off the roots and
remove the tops and outer skin if necessary.
Split them lengthways and lay half of them on an
oval plate or dish large enough to take the fish.
Peel and thinly slice the ginger and garlic, lay a
few slices on top of the spring onions, and a few
slices in the fish. Put the fish in the dish and
sprinkle the remaining ginger and garlic on top.
Cover with more spring onions. Pour over a
tablespoon of soy sauce and place in a steamer.
Steam for 8-12 minutes. Boil up the rest of the
soy sauce, the sherry and sesame oil. Remove the
fish from the steamer, uncover it, put the spring
onions around it and pour the hot soy mixture
over the fish. Serve immediately.

TAIWAN

TAIPEI

The image I have of this strange city that remains the strongest is a food-related one, but not in the way that you might imagine. It is the recollection of a small aubergine, exquisitely carved in a soft, translucent greenish white jadeite, displayed alone in a glass case, among far more imposing religious jades, chi-chi or 'worship objects', and jade tablets from the T'ang and Sung dynasties. This small jade ornament probably came from the later Sung or Yuan dynasties, by which time jade carving had taken on a more personal, realistic and simple character, drawing on everyday life for birds and flowers, fruit, vegetables, landscapes and human figures. It is one of the most beautiful objects I have ever seen, one of the few things I have ever really coveted.

The extraordinary National Palace Museum where you can find the jade aubergine is a replica of Beijing's Forbidden City. The imperial style architecture sits well against the green, fresh hillside on which it is situated well outside Taipei. A collection of some 700,000 pieces is housed there, representing 5,000 years of Chinese history, complete and unbroken, right up to 1949, when this huge treasure was taken from China by the Kuomintang. Underground caverns store much of it, for only a fraction is exhibited at one time. It can be an exhausting place and we went to look at only a few of the rooms; the flower paintings, the ritual bronzes, an exhibition devoted to the development of calligraphy, Ch'ing Dynasty costume accessories, the Ting ware white porcelain and, of course, the jade.

If you pick a weekday morning you will be able to enjoy a calm unhurried visit and then be able to rest and refresh yourself in the beautiful tea room on the top floor of the museum, which is designed as a replica of a noble lord's music room. Songbirds in rosewood cages sing while you sip fine rose congou or po lih tea and nibble sweet bean paste cakes and steamed char siu bao (barbecued pork dumplings). You will probably also be tempted by the antique tea sets for sale – small, smooth pots and tiny, almost doll-size handleless cups, made from a deep violet-brown clay.

Our visit to the National Museum was but a brief respite from our stay in this noisy, ugly polluted city in 1988. For Taipei is all of

94

those things. The ride in from Chiang Kai-Shek airport, all 30 kilometres of it, is one of the least lovely in the world. Urban and industrial sprawl, if not squalor, are very soon upon you, and a thick heavy blanket of smog lies over the city. Much of this comes from the thousands of mopeds that are the main form of transport, which together with rash cyclists and old overcrowded buses that clash gears, pull out without signalling and jolt to a sudden halt, make crossing the road a hazardous business and walking the main streets not a particularly pleasant or relaxing occupation. Pedestrian footbridges built high across the busiest roads help, but you do well to slap a large handkerchief across nose and mouth before crossing. At that level the fumes and dirt seem just as bad.

Taxis are the most efficient form of transport and relatively inexpensive. Among the paper ephemera I kept from our visit to Taipei is a taxi check list. It lists all the places that a visitor could possibly want to visit, including the Martyrs' Shrine, the Grand Hotel, and the Lungshan Temple, in both English and Mandarin, with a space for you to tick. There is also a card which informs the dear guest, "The taxi you are now riding in bears the followng number plate. Please retain this ticket in case any problem may arise from the ride." This is handed to you by the hotel doorman, who has ostentatiously made a note of the taxi's licence plate. When we investigated we learnt that the government, in an effort to encourage tourism, was trying to stamp out bad practices among taxi drivers. In the whole time we were there we never experienced any problems, so perhaps the deterrent is working.

If this makes Taipei sound like a difficult city, it is. And yet, if you persevere, get off into the side streets, see the temples and the night markets, and eat in the excellent restaurants, the rewards are more worthwhile because hard won. The oriental charm is well hidden beneath the hustle and bustle of the growing city, but it is there. Shemending, the area behind and to the west of the Hilton, used to be a quiet residential area of attractive old houses. Much of it is now noisy, gaudy and teeming with the young of Taipei clustering around music and clothes shops, cinemas and fast food outlets. All spill out on to the uneven pavements and each shop has a different and highly efficient sound system booming forth.

Following one of the lanes between Wuchang Street and Omei Street, past a small street temple where you can light a joss stick, we found a tiny oasis of calm, the Shen Shyh Coffee Shop. And it was indeed a coffee shop, a cross between a Dutch brown café and an old-fashioned coffee bar. Smiles and gestures brought us, again unexpectedly, frothy cappuccino. Back in the noise of the street once more we wandered past food stalls from which wafted pungent appetizing smells. Some of the stalls cooked food for you after you had picked out what you wanted from the things displayed. Other stalls sold food for the home cook; there were pickle stalls, noodle stalls and those with rack upon rack of dried squid. The fruit and vegetable stalls were piled with healthy looking, luscious fresh produce, loquats, star fruit, papaya, mandarins and, something I had not seen before, rose apples. Their name is entirely descriptive and the fruit look for all the world like those perfect wax fruits the Victorians were fond of displaying under glass domes. The covered market not far from the Lung Shan temple is a maze of cool, dark alleys. Meat, fish, clothes, jewellery, fruit, eggs, vegetables, shoes, all jostle together in a close promiscuity.

Hunger led us to Umeco or the May Garden restaurant on the third floor at No. 1 Lane 107, Lin Shen North Road. This is a simple, clean bright place with pleasant service where we ate a marvellous and unusual meal. The glutinous rice bowl came with mixed roast meats, peanuts cooked soft, roast peanut powder, pickled radish and coriander. It was a most savoury and appetizing combination. What came next was described in English as fried leeks and beancurd, but I'm convinced it was garlic chives. The fried egg and turnip was like a delicately textured yet earthy flavoured frittata. The grilled squid, so plainly cooked, was sweet, subtle, tender and charred. Peanuts showed themselves again in the sweet, a sticky marshmallow dipped in roasted peanut flour. With the meal we drank local beer.

There is a huge variety of restaurants to choose from and many who know say that you can still eat the best Chinese food in Taiwan. Fast food has hit the city in a big way however, from the burger outlets to the food courts, which are indoor street food markets with good standards of hygiene. There is a basement food court next to the Taipei Hilton called the FM Station, and here different stalls sell Japanese, Italian, Szechuan, Taiwanese and Cantonese snacks and meals, fruit juices and ice creams, which you can eat at central tables. It is not a bad way to sample a range of local delicacies if you are wary of the street stalls.

As in other cities in the Far East, hotel food in Taipei can be excellent. Inside the Hilton itself is Hunan Heaven, a small, elegant yet comfortable restaurant, with several private banqueting rooms off it. The walls are covered in pastel silk, the furniture is rich lacquered rosewood. But most striking of all are the wall decorations, breathtaking antique ceremonial imperial costumes from the Chin, Han, Sung and Ching dynasties. These museum pieces are carefully displayed and greatly enhanced our enjoyment of the exquisite classical food we were served. The Hilton in Taipei has a long tradition of excellence. The legendary James Smith used to be General Manager there and his wife Julia (who later succeeded him as GM) the Food and Beverage Manager. Together, with the help of Stanley Huang and Wen-Shan Yu, who are both still there, they put together and published a very good book on Chinese culinary heritage.

Fine food still comes out of those kitchens. Wen-Shan Yu devised for us a banquet of classical Hunan specialities, including braised shark's fin with crab roe, smoked pomfret Hunan-style, which I have to say tasted awfully like kippers, and steamed beef brisket soup with yellow fungi served in bamboo cups. The *pièce de résistance* was the lamb vagabond king, a recipe for which appears on p. 124. It is a dish that has evolved from the traditional beggar's chicken and I feel it deserves a place in everyone's repertoire. The cooking method is rather special.

Another restaurant not to be missed is the busy Shin Yeh Tatung in Shuang Cheng Street. This is a Taiwanese restaurant near the President Hotel. Go there for dinner and spend time first wandering round the night market stalls. I remember watching a woman carefully arranging fruit in a tray. The strawberries were so perfect they looked handpainted. The main shopping street is nearby with its department stores. The little lanes running off it are full of coffee shops, pastry shops, restaurants and European style bars and pubs. The food at the Shin Yeh is earthy and robust with masses of flavour and texture. It was crowded the evening we were there. As with all the restaurants in Taipei the menu is very easy to order from since there are pictures of the food and fairly comprehensible English translations. We drank beer and ate fried beancurd in a brown sauce and pork with sour cabbage, fried greens, rice and chicken and lily flower soup. A waitress brought by a dish of drunken prawns to be cooked at the next table. They (the prawns) were indeed inebriated but not taking it lying down. One jumped out of the dish of rice wine and began skeetering across the floor. As with everywhere we travelled in our search for all the Chinas, the emphasis was firmly on freshness.

Taipei is one of the strangest places we have ever visited. It is hard to explain why it felt more foreign than China, but it did. Disturbing images still remain. The anti-aircraft posts on the outskirts of the city were not monuments to some forgotten war, but ready for use, painted in camouflage with guns pointing to the sky and aiming west. Near the Memorial to the Martyrs is one of the sights of Taipei: the Grand Hotel. Built in massive imperial style, all red and gold, it is a most magnificent building, with inlaid floors, fine rosewood panelling and furniture, woven silk washed carpets, high ceilings, wide staircases and beautiful gardens. And it is sufficiently away from the city centre to have fresh air. It is indeed a hotel, the literature in the foyer and at the reception desk says so. It offers all the usual services, sports facilities, coffee shop, banquets and receptions, baby sitting, and barber shop. You can speak to the management on extension 1144 and reserve a table in the Ming Grill on extension 1106. But I'm far from sure that one can actually stay there. You hear stories of people making a booking and then arriving to find that "the hotel is full". It is said to be owned by Madam Chiang Kai-shek's family and to be used only for official guests of the government.

$\mathcal{M}$EAT

STIR-FRIED CHICKEN *With* CELERIAC AND MUSHROOMS

While celeriac is a favourite addition to casseroles and makes a traditional slow-cooked braised vegetable to serve with game or roast beef, it also lends itself well to a simple stir-fry. The flavour given to the rest of the ingredients is that of celery, but the texture is quite different. It is important to slice it thinly for quick cooking. Pork tenderloin can be used instead of chicken.

Serves 4-6

3 × 140 g/5 oz boneless,
   skinless chicken breasts
4 tbsp dry Amontillado sherry or rice wine
• pinch of five-spice powder
   or ground fennel
340 g/12 oz celeriac bulb
  1 carrot
110 g/4 oz shiitake, oyster
   or cultivated mushrooms
3-4 spring onions or baby leeks
  3 cloves garlic
  2 tbsp sunflower oil for frying
1-2 tbsp soy sauce
  2 tsp toasted sesame oil
  2 tsp toasted sesame seeds

Cut the chicken into oblique strips, no more than 1 cm/½ inch thick and about 4 cm/ 1½ inches long. Marinate them in the wine and spices and put to one side while you prepare the vegetables. Peel and slice the celeriac then cut it into fine strips, or shave it into strips with a potato peeler. Deal with the carrot in the same way. Wipe the mushrooms and slice them. Trim and slice the onions or leeks and peel and crush the garlic. With a slotted spoon remove the chicken from its marinade and let this drip back into the bowl for use later on. Dry the chicken on paper towels.

Heat the sunflower oil in a wok or fryingpan and when it is hot, stir in the chicken pieces. Add the celeriac and carrots after 2-3 minutes, and stir-fry these for a few minutes more. Add the mushrooms, spring onions or leeks and garlic. Stir continuously for another couple of minutes or so and then put the lid on to let it all steam for another few minutes. Add 2 tablespoons water, the soy sauce and oil, stir to blend all the flavours then turn out into a serving dish. Scatter on the sesame seeds, which you can toast by heating them gently in a heavy fryingpan. This is very good served with crisp green vegetables such as broccoli, green beans or Chinese flowering cabbage (choy sum).

HONEY-GRILLED CHICKEN
With PARSNIPS

A sweetened glaze will encourage even more caramelization under the grill, which will give a tasty, crisp finish to the chicken skin. The natural sweetness in the parsnips will cause them to caramelize lightly too, as they are browned under the grill. Use a small chicken, about 680 g/1½ lb maximum, that is the largest poussin size. The parsnips should be young and tender, not the old woody kind.

Serves 2

1 chicken
3 tbsp clear honey
1 tbsp soy sauce
- a few drops of sesame oil
2 cloves garlic, crushed or chopped small
- a few drops of chilli oil or Tabasco sauce
- freshly ground black pepper
225 g/8 oz young parsnips

Cut the wing tips from the bird. Remove any excess fat. With a pair of kitchen scissors or a heavy knife, cut along and remove the backbone and open the bird out flat. Wipe all over with kitchen paper. Mix the rest of the ingredients together except the parsnips and brush liberally over the chicken, skin side only. Peel the parsnips and cut into very thin slices, length-ways. Heat the grill to full. Place the chicken, skin side down, and the parsnip slices on the grill rack. Grill under full heat for 2-3 minutes, then turn down and grill under moderate heat for 8 minutes. Turn the chicken and parsnip over and grill under full heat for 3-4 minutes, then turn down and cook for a few minutes more. The chicken will need a little longer than the parsnips.

This is good served with plain rice and a few stir-fried vegetables.

DEEP-FRIED CHICKEN
PARCELS

I have tried to re-create this dish from one we ate at Hsieh's Garden in Singapore. Rarely do I deep-fry anything but these succulent parcels oozing fragrant juices when you open them are well worth it. Finger bowls and extra napkins are essential.

Serves 4

680 g/1½ lb chicken joints, chopped
    into 5 cm/2 inch pieces
4 tbsp Shaoxing wine
    or Amontillado sherry
2 tsp honey
1 tsp grated ginger
½ tsp ground cinnamon
½ tsp ground coriander
- pinch five-spice powder
- pinch Szechuan pepper
2 tbsp grated orange zest
2 tbsp soy sauce
1 tbsp sesame oil
2 spring onions, thinly sliced
15 cm/6 inch squares of greaseproof
    paper
- oil for frying

GARNISH
- bean sprouts, spring onions
   and coriander

Moisten the chicken pieces with half the wine and the honey then sprinkle with the dry ingredients. Mix the soy sauce and sesame oil with the remaining wine and pour over the chicken. Scatter over the spring onion. Cover and marinate overnight. Next day, wrap each piece of chicken in a piece of greaseproof paper, making sure that it is well sealed by pinching and folding the edges. Heat the oil in a wok or deep pan to 180°C/330°F and lower in the parcels. Fry for 8-10 minutes, drain and pile up on a platter. Garnish with greenery and serve.

GINSENG AND MUSHROOM CHICKEN

A wonderfully soothing dish, best served with plain boiled or steamed rice, this is the perfect "bringing you back from the brink" food. Whether you are jet-lagged, suffering the aftermath of flu and a rotten journey home or a broken love-affair, this dish of poached chicken with its healthgiving broth will set the world to rights again. My sister-in-law Bettina taught me how to cook it. Her mother swears by it as having real medicinal value. Use a free-range chicken if you possibly can.

Serves 6-8

1.35-1.8 kg/3-4 lb free-range chicken
2-3 ginseng roots, broken in two
  1 celery stalk
  1 Chinese radish
  1 carrot
2-3 star anise
  1 tsp Szechuan pepper
  8 dried flower mushrooms
  5 cm/2 inch piece fresh ginger,
    peeled and sliced

Trim any excess fat from the chicken and put one of the ginseng roots in the cavity. Put the chicken in a large casserole or stockpot. Peel and trim the vegetables and slice or cut into batons, but not too small. Put these around the chicken, together with the star anise, the rest of the ginseng, pepper, mushrooms and ginger. Cover the chicken with plenty of cold water. Bring to the boil, skim, and reduce the heat as low as possible. Poach the chicken for 2-2½ hours. Serve in large soup plates a few pieces of chicken, vegetables, a piece of ginseng and some broth poured over it. Bowls of rice can be served separately.

Overleaf: Honey-grilled Chicken with Parsnips; Garlic Chives with Bacon (p. 153)

CHICKEN HAINAN-STYLE

Popular all over Southeast Asia wherever there are Chinese cooks, this dish makes a very good main course for an informal lunch or dinner. It originated on Hainan, the large tropical island off the southwest coast of China, but you are as likely to be served it in Singapore as in Shanghai.

You need the *very* best chicken you can find, preferably free-range. The chicken is poached and eaten cool or cold with freshly boiled rice and hot broth. It is best to cook the chicken in the morning to eat later in the day. It does not taste nearly as good if it comes from the refrigerator, but nor should it be left cooling at room temperature for more than two hours. This will serve 4-6 people as a main course, more if part of a Chinese meal.

Serves 4-6

1.8 kg/4 lb chicken
1 tsp five-spice powder
6 star anise pods
12 peppercorns, roughly crushed
1 medium onion stuck with 6 cloves
6 fresh coriander stalks (use the
  leaves for garnish)
6 thin slices fresh ginger root
7.5 cm/3 inch piece cinnamon stick
2 tbsp rice wine or Amontillado sherry
2 tbsp soy sauce

Rinse the chicken thoroughly, inside and out, remove any fat and cut off the wing pinions. If it has been trussed remove the string to allow it to cook through more evenly. Place the chicken in a large saucepan, cover it with water, and add the rest of the ingredients. Bring to the boil over medium heat, skim off any impurities which rise to the surface, cover and poach very gently, that is, with the occasional bubble just breaking on the surface, for 35 minutes.

Remove the pan from the heat, and allow the chicken to cool in the stock. The initial residual heat will easily complete the cooking of the chicken. After 1½ hours, remove the chicken from the stock, reserving the stock, and plunge it into a large bowl full of water and ice cubes for 10 minutes. This will set the juices in the chicken to a clear jelly. Remove the chicken from the ice, and then chop, cut or cleave it into neat pieces of a size to be picked up by chopsticks. Arrange on a dish, and garnish with coriander and extra star anise.

The accompanying dishes can be prepared while the chicken is cooking. Cook some long-grain rice in twice its volume of stock or water. Garnish with thinly sliced and fried onion. Grate a 7.5 cm/3 inch piece of fresh ginger, mix with a teaspoon of sea salt and serve in a small bowl. Another condiment can be made by mixing some chilli sauce or chopped chillies with garlic, oil and rice vinegar. In a third bowl mix equal quantities of soy sauce and rice vinegar with a teaspoon of toasted sesame oil. The stock, once you have removed the chicken, can be boiled, strained and served in bowls with some shredded spring onion.

EAST MEETS WEST CHICKEN

This fanciful name describes a dish I devised after a successful shopping trip in Soho. Fresh English corn-fed chicken, French tarragon and vividly fresh Chinese vegetables – choy sum and garlic chives. The chicken was stuffed and then steamed and served with a sauce made of dried mushrooms in a reduced fumet enriched with crème fraîche and butter. The vegetables were steamed too.

Serves 4

8 dried shiitake mushrooms
4 plump chicken breasts
- seasoning, including a pinch
of nutmeg
170 g/6 oz cottage cheese
2 tbsp chopped fresh herbs
60 ml/2 fl oz crème fraîche
or Greek yogurt
15 g/½ oz unsalted butter

VEGETABLE ACCOMPANIMENTS

225-340 g/8-12 oz green vegetables
such as choy sum, bok choy or broccoli
- chives to garnish; garlic chives
if you can find them

Two or three hours in advance, put the dried mushrooms in a basin and pour on 300 ml/ 10 fl oz boiling water to soften them. Skin and trim the chicken breasts and cut a deep slit in each to form a pocket for stuffing, taking care not to pierce it. Season the chicken lightly. Place the cottage cheese in a sieve and rinse it thoroughly. Odd though it may sound, this is the best way to obtain a dry cottage cheese. Shake it in the sieve and let it drain. When no more liquid drips from it, sieve the cheese into a clean basin and mix the chopped herbs with it. Divide the mixture into four and stuff each chicken breast, securing it with cocktail sticks. Place the chicken breasts in a lightly oiled steamer basket. In another steamer basket, lay the washed and prepared vegetables. The chicken will take 12-15 minutes to steam, the vegetables 5-8 minutes. Put the chicken on to steam as you serve the first course, or even during it depending on how fast or slowly the meal is to be eaten.

Meanwhile, prepare the sauce. Put the mushrooms and their liquid in a small saucepan, bring to the boil and simmer gently until the mushrooms are tender. This can take 20-30 minutes depending on how long they have soaked, their size and age. Reduce the cooking liquor by two thirds. Add the cream and stir thoroughly. Season to taste.

Steam the chicken breasts, and then the vegetables. Stir the butter into the sauce, beating thoroughly to amalgamate it. Arrange a chicken breast on each heated dinner plate, with some of the vegetables neatly placed beside it. Spoon sauce into the centre of the plate and arrange the mushrooms on the sauce. Garnish with long lengths of chives and serve immediately.

Overleaf: Deep-fried Chicken Parcels (p. 100)

FRIED MARINATED QUAILS
With CRISP MINT LEAVES

The first time I was invited into Ah Chan's kitchen at the Fung Lum in Shatin he cooked pigeon for our table. The plump tender squabs available in Hong Kong are very different from our dark, gamey and, it has to be said, usually tough wood pigeons, which would not be at all suitable for this cooking treatment. Instead I use quails. The deep-fried mint leaves served as an edible garnish are very effective but do add to your time in the kitchen since they should be done at the last minute if they are not to go soggy.

Serves 4

- 4 oven-ready quails, boned or not, as you prefer
- salt and pepper
- 4 star anise pods
- 1 tbsp soy sauce
- 2 tbsp rice wine
- 1 tbsp clear honey
- good pinch ground Szechuan pepper
- about 500 ml/18 fl oz groundnut oil for frying
- bunch of fresh mint, rinsed and thoroughly dried, and each leaf or sprig separated

Lightly season the quails and put a star anise in each cavity. Put the quails in a shallow dish. Mix the soy sauce, rice wine, honey and pepper and pour it over the quails, turning them so that they are well covered with the marinade. Cover and refrigerate for at least 3 hours, or overnight if this is more convenient. Gently heat a wok and pour in the oil. Remove the quails from the marinade and let any liquid drip back into the dish. Pat them dry. When the oil is hot, put in the quails and fry them, turning them from time to time for about 12-15 minutes until, when pierced with a skewer, the juices run clear. Remove them from the oil and drain them on kitchen paper, then put them on a serving plate and keep them in a warm place.

Reheat the oil and fry the mint leaves, in batches if necessary, until they are dark green, crisp and transparent. The oil should be hotter than for the quails since the leaves are only going to be in it for 30 seconds or so. Take out the mint leaves with a slotted spoon. Pour the oil away or strain it for reuse. Reheat the wok and add 4 tablespoons water. When it has nearly evaporated add any remaining marinade or an extra splash of rice wine and soy sauce. Swirl around the pan and pour over the quails. Garnish with fried mint leaves.

Serve with a cucumber salad (see p. 60) or green salad or steamed green vegetables and rice.

NOTE Basil leaves can be fried instead of mint leaves.

QUAIL IN BAMBOO TUBE

At the Cherry Garden restaurant at the Oriental in Singapore, which specializes in Hunan cooking, master chef Huang Ching Biào, originally from Taiwan, serves a wonderful dish made from finely minced pigeon steamed and served in sections of bamboo tube. This functional and attractive "oven-to-table" ware is not easy to find in the West. Straight-sided ramekins or smallish soufflé dishes will suffice, the deeper the better, or any other heatproof beaker-like container. You can also cook the soup in a single pot, such as the brown glazed Dutch oven.

The pigeon used in Chinese cooking is not our gamey wood pigeon but the much more delicate squab. Free-range chicken, duckling or quail can be used instead in the recipe which I have adapted from Ah Huang's.

Serves 4

225 g/8 oz quail (breast meat)
30 g/1 oz water chestnut
1 slice Parma or other cured ham
450 ml/15 fl oz water
- good pinch of salt
- pinch of white pepper
- 1 tbsp rice wine or Amontillado sherry

Remove the skin from the quail breasts, and mince them very fine, using a processor, a mincer or two cleavers on a chopping block. Chop the water chestnut very finely but without reducing it to a paste. Shred the ham as finely as possible. Mix these ingredients together in a bowl. Add the water, seasoning and rice wine. Thoroughly mix and divide amongst the four dishes or ramekins. Place carefully on a rack in a steamer, and steam for 35-40 minutes. The dish is cooked when the meat rises to the surface, soft, tender and delicate with a rich broth underneath.

QUAIL IN SPICED JELLY

This makes a marvellous picnic dish if transported in a refrigerated box, so that the jelly remains as it is rather than turning to a liquid. The quails can, of course, be served hot, when they are delicious with the garlic rice on p. 67.

Serves 8

8 oven-ready quails
2 tbsp soy sauce
1 tsp five-spice powder
1 tbsp groundnut oil
2 finely chopped shallots
2-3 pieces of lemon grass
140 ml/5 fl oz dry white wine
- seasoning

Trim and tie the quails neatly if they have not already been trussed. Rub them all over with the soy sauce and spices and let them stand for half an hour or so. Heat the oil and fry the shallots without browning them. Break each piece of lemon grass into three or four, and insert a piece into the cavity of each bird. Fry the quails until browned all over. Add the rest of the lemon grass and the white wine, bring to the boil, then simmer with the lid on, or place in a medium oven, for 25 minutes. When done, place the quails in a shallow earthenware or china dish, strain the pan juices over them, season lightly and allow them to cool. Cover and refrigerate if necessary until required.

Overleaf: Quail in Spiced Jelly; Crisp Cucumber (p. 60)

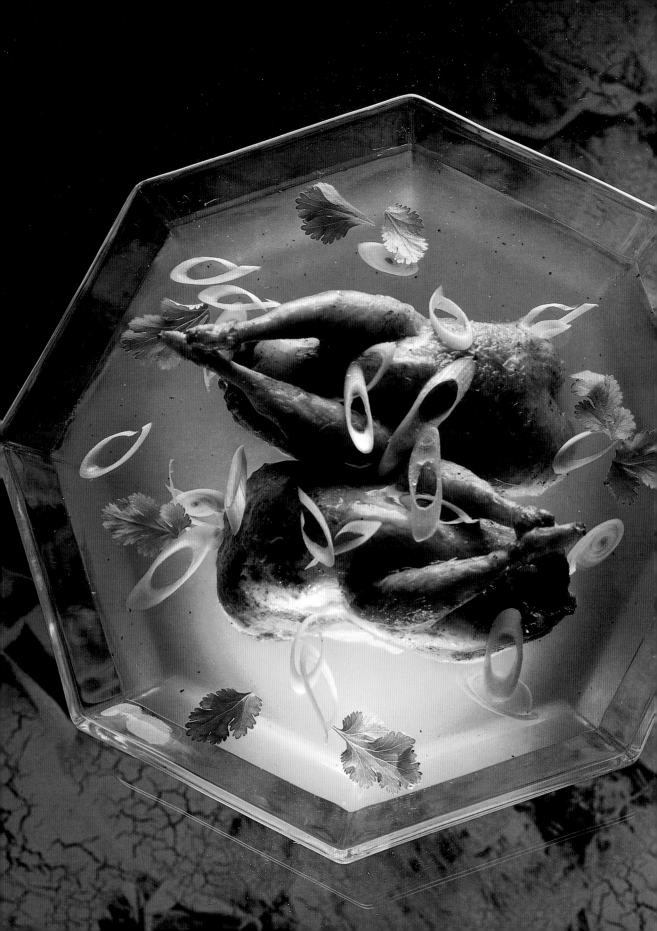

ROAST TURKEY

Ken Hom provided the inspiration for this alternative offering for the Christmas table. He has a unique way of carving turkey. Instead of serving long thin slices of breast meat he removes the breast in its entirety and chops it with a cleaver into thick juicy steaks.

If you can, get an oven-ready farm fresh turkey, and ask for a Cambridge Bronze or Norfolk Black. They have a great deal of flavour. A bird about 4.5 kg/10 lb will feed 6-8 people amply, giving two thighs, two drumsticks, two wings and six or eight pieces from the breast. Serve the bird with the stir-fried ginger sprouts on p. 155, garlic wild rice on p. 68 and braised celery on p. 152 for a delicious, alternative Christmas dinner.

Serves 6-8

4.5 kg/10 lb turkey, plus giblets
 1 smallish onion
 1 celery stalk
 1 leek
 1 carrot
 2 stalks of lemon grass
2.5 cm/1 inch chunk fresh ginger
 4 cloves
 4 cloves garlic
7.5 cm/3 inch piece cinnamon stick
 4 tbsp soy sauce
140 ml/5 fl oz Shaoxing wine
  or Amontillado sherry
 1 tbsp clear honey
 1 tbsp toasted sesame oil
 1 tbsp rice vinegar
 2 tsp ground Szechuan pepper

Trim any excess fat from the cavity and make sure you have removed all the giblets. You can reserve the the liver to use in another dish, but use the rest to make a rich stock which will form the basis of the gravy for the turkey. Brown the giblets all over, then cover with plenty of water and simmer. To the pot add the clean peelings from the onion, celery, leek and carrot, and a little of the outer leaves of the lemon grass and the ginger peelings. Stick the cloves in the onion and put all the vegetables, roughly chopped or sliced, in the bottom of a roasting tin lightly brushed with oil. Put the garlic, lemon grass and cinnamon inside the turkey. Mix the liquid ingredients and the Szechuan pepper and brush this all over the bird, inside and out.

Place the turkey on top of the vegetables, breast side down, and cover completely but loosely with foil. Roast in a preheated oven at 180°C/350°F, gas mark 4 for 3½ hours. Baste the bird every hour. After 2 hours turn it breast side up, and after 3 hours remove the foil to brown the breast. Test for thorough cooking by piercing the deepest part of the thigh with a larding needle. The juices should run clear. There is no merit, in fact there is positive danger, in serving a turkey undercooked.

While the turkey is cooking, attend to the gravy by reducing the turkey stock to about 300 ml/10 fl oz and straining into it any marinade that is left. When you remove the turkey from the oven, it should be kept covered in a warm place for at least 20 minutes before attempting to carve it. Carefully drain any cooking juices into the gravy pan. Reduce further if required, but be careful not to reduce it to the point of over-saltiness. Strain into a heated jug or gravy boat and hand separately.

MINCED QUAIL
With LETTUCE

This dish is a variation on one to be found on the menus of smart Chinese restaurants in Hong Kong and Britain. It is, nevertheless, a simple dish to prepare and makes a good snack or starter for a dinner party. Tender young spinach is another suitable leaf for wrapping. Blanched leaves of chard or older spinach are good too, but lack the contrasting crunch of raw leaves. The ordinary iceberg lettuce is most suitable, or a Webb. Cos is difficult because of the firm centre ribs.

Serves 4

As a starter

  4 *quails*
  1 *tbsp groundnut oil*
2-3 *cloves garlic*
  1 *tbsp soy sauce*
  5 *tbsp rice wine or dry sherry*
  1 *good pinch ground anise*
    or five-spice powder
  3 *spring onions, chopped*
  2 *tsp Worcester sauce*
  ● *few drops Angostura bitters*
12 *large lettuce leaves*

DIPPING MIXTURE

4 *tbsp soy sauce*
1 *tsp Worcester sauce*   *mixed*
1 *tsp rice vinegar or* *together*
  sherry vinegar

Remove feet and neck from quails if this has not already been done. Heat the oil in a heavy saucepan or casserole and fry the quails all over until well browned. Crush the garlic and add to the pan with the rest of the ingredients except the lettuce leaves. Cover and cook the quails on a low heat on top of the stove for 25 minutes or so until done. Remove them from the pan. Carefully remove the legs and return these to the pan to marinate in the cooking juices. Remove the breasts and chop or mince the meat quite finely. Best not to process it as it produces too smooth a mixture. The meat should be fairly loose textured and crumbly, but you can moisten it with a little of the cooking juices. Heap the meat on to a plate. Arrange the legs around the edge. Boil up the cooking juices until syrupy and spoon over the legs. Hand the meat around with the lettuce leaves and the dipping mixture.

Overleaf: Roast Barbary Duck (p. 116)

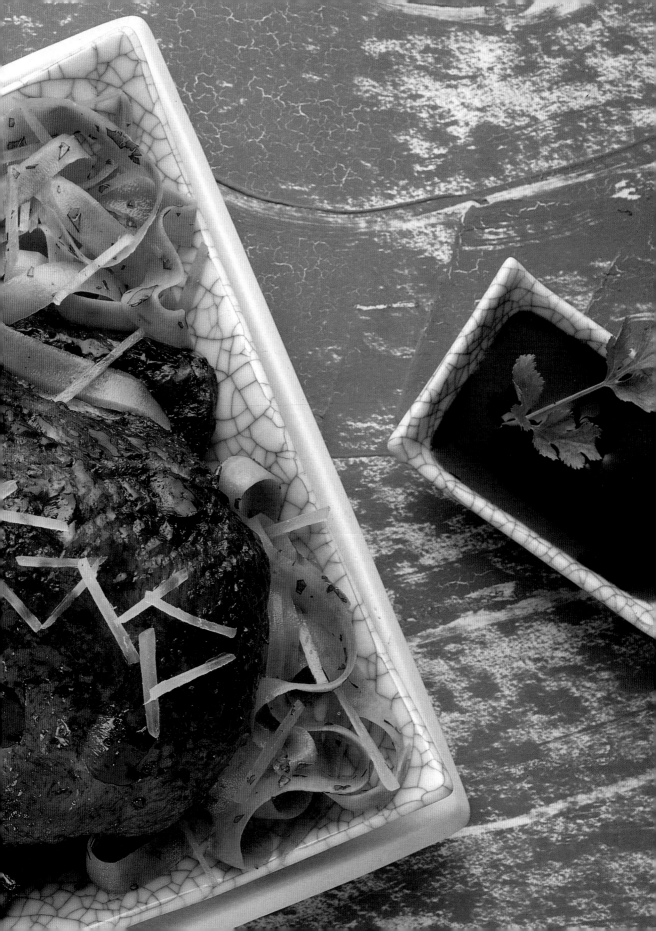

PIGEON BREASTS *With* SWEET *AND* SOUR VEGETABLES

Serves 4

4 plump tender pigeons
• ground black pepper
6-8 crushed juniper berries
  2 celery hearts or 6 sticks celery
225 g/8 oz Chinese cabbage
  2 carrots
  2 leeks
170 g/6 oz fresh oyster or shiitake mushrooms
  2 tsp soy sauce
  1 tsp brown sugar
  2 tsp rice vinegar

Carefully remove the breasts from the pigeons. Brown the rest of the carcases in a heavy saucepan and add 570 ml/1 pint water and the trimmings from the vegetables; simmer gently until you have a rich tasty stock. Season the breasts with freshly ground black pepper and the crushed juniper berries.

Peel and finely slice or shred the vegetables. Place in a steamer basket with the mushrooms on top and steam until tender but not soggy.

Meanwhile cook the pigeon breasts, either in a non-stick frying pan, a well seasoned cast-iron pan or under a hot grill for 3-4 minutes on each side. Allow to rest in a warm place on a plate. When the vegetables are cooked, tip them into a bowl. Mix the soy sauce, sugar and vinegar and stir this into the vegetables until they are well coated and the sugar has melted. Divide between four heated dinner plates. Slice each breast in two, and arrange four slices on each plate, pouring over any cooking juices collected on the plate.

ROAST BARBARY DUCK

*T*his is a perfect centrepiece for a celebration dinner for two.

Serves 2

1.35 kg/3 lb Barbary duck
2-3 cloves garlic
  2 tbsp soy sauce
  1 tbsp sesame oil
  1 tsp chilli oil
  2 tbsp rice wine
  1 tbsp clear honey
  1 tbsp rice vinegar
  1 small fennel bulb
  2 carrots
  1 celery stalk
2.5 cm/1 inch piece fresh ginger
  4 star anise pods
  1 piece dried orange or tangerine peel
140 ml/5 fl oz stock or good white wine

STUFFING

• the liver, gizzard and heart of the bird
  2 tbsp melted butter
170 g/6 oz cooked rice; if possible, a mixture of brown, wild and basmati rice
  1 celery stalk, finely chopped
  1 small onion, peeled and finely chopped
  2 garlic cloves, crushed
  1 small apple, peeled and grated
  1 tbsp sultanas
  1 tbsp pine kernels or chopped almonds
  1 tbsp chopped crystallized ginger
  6 cloves
• good pinch of five-spice powder
• salt and pepper

Cut the wing pinions from the duck. Insert garlic slivers into the skin. Mix the soy sauce, oils, rice wine, honey and vinegar and brush over the duck, reserving the rest. The duck can be brushed with the marinade and left overnight, covered and refrigerated. Peel and slice the vegetables thinly, including the ginger root, and place in the bottom of the roasting pan with the star anise and the peel. Prick the duck all over, particularly in the fatty parts.

Make the stuffing. Chop the giblets very small, and fry them in half the butter. Allow to cool, then mix with the rest of the ingredients. Spoon into the body cavity and secure with cocktail sticks.

Place the duck on the vegetables breast down. Roast in a preheated oven, 200°C/400°F, gas mark 6, for about 1½ hours. After half an hour, remove from the oven, and carefully drain off the fat. Brush on a little more of the soy sauce mixture, and pour a couple of spoonfuls of stock on to the vegetables. Do this again half an hour later. When cooked, keep the duck warm while you finish the sauce. Drain off the rest of the fat. Pour the rest of the stock or wine into the roasting pan, and place on top of the stove. Bring to the boil, scraping up any bits stuck to the bottom of the tin. Add a little water, if necessary. Taste and adjust the seasoning. Strain into a jug, and serve with the duck.

ROAST SADDLE OF RABBIT STUFFED With TOFU AND CHINESE GREENS

Have the butcher leave the saddle whole. Use the legs for pâté or in a casserole. Buy two rabbits if you want to serve four as a main course.

Serves 2

1 large saddle of rabbit
• salt, pepper
1 bunch garlic chives
60 g/2 oz ong choy
110 g/4 oz medium-firm tofu
2 tsp Chinese mustard
2 cloves garlic, peeled and crushed
2 tsp finely chopped crystallized ginger

Bone the saddle by cutting with a sharp knife on each side of the backbone and scraping along and down over the ribs, easing the flesh off the bones. When you have finished you should have two long fillets of lean meat, each with a thin flap. Season the meat lightly and lay one piece next to the other, flaps overlapping. Wash and dry the vegetables. Remove any damaged or yellowing leaves and the coarsest stalks. Finely chop and mix with the crumbled tofu and mustard. Add the crushed garlic and ginger. Spoon the mixture on to the flap and spread evenly. Slip 4 or 5 lengths of twine under the meat, bring the two edges together and tie together as a roll in 4 or 5 places, making sure that the filling is not oozing out of the ends. Slip the meat inside a roasting bag, slit in one or two places. Secure it tightly and place on a baking sheet in a preheated oven, 180°C/350°F, gas mark 4, and roast for 25 minutes.

Remove from the oven and allow it to rest in a warm place for 10 minutes before slicing into neat rounds and serving with any cooking juices and some vegetables. I like to serve something green and crisp, like squeaky beans or crunchy broccoli and something soft like a parsnip and potato purée, or a bowl of rice.

BEANCURD-STUFFED PORK ROLLS BRAISED *With* SPICED CABBAGE

This is a flavoursome winter dish which makes use of store-cupboard spices rather than fresh ones.

Serves 4

2 tbsp groundnut oil
455 g/1 lb shredded savoy
     or winter cabbage
1 mild onion, peeled and sliced
● good pinch Szechuan peppercorns
● good pinch dried lemon grass
● good pinch dried galangal
1 tbsp rice wine
1 tbsp muscovado sugar
8 thin pork escalopes
     about 70 g/2½ oz each
● groundnut oil for frying

STUFFING

4 soaked Chinese mushrooms
1 piece soaked wood ear mushroom
2 shallots or 4 spring onions, peeled
60 g/2 oz bean sprouts or Yam bean
170 g/6 oz beancurd
     (not silken tofu), crumbled
60 g/2 oz cooked ham,
     diced or shredded
● pinch ground coriander
2 tsp soy sauce
2 tsp egg white

GARNISH

● fresh coriander leaves

Prepare the cabbage first. Heat the oil and stir-fry the cabbage and onion with the spices for about 5 minutes. Stir in the rice wine and sugar. Spread the mixture in an ovenproof dish. For the stuffing, finely chop all the vegetables and mix them with the crumbled beancurd, ham and coriander. Mix in the soy sauce and then the egg white to bind the stuffing. Flatten the escalopes and divide the stuffing between them. Roll up into neat parcels so that the stuffing does not escape. Secure with thread or cocktail sticks. Fry the rolls all over, then arrange them on top of the cabbage. Cover with oiled foil and bake in the bottom half of a warm oven, 170°C/325°F, gas mark 3, for about 2 hours.

Serve with potatoes, rice or noodles and garnish with fresh coriander.

ROAST PORK TENDERLOIN
With
ORIENTAL FLAVOURS

Cooking the tenderloin in a roasting bag will keep this leanest of all pork cuts juicy and tender. For extra flavour, marinate the meat overnight. Serve it with plain steamed or boiled rice and stir-fried mixed vegetables. Use lemon or anise flavouring, not both. To serve four people, buy two tenderloins and double the rest of the ingredients.

Serves 2

- 1 pork tenderloin, weighing about 400 g/14 oz
- 3 cloves garlic, peeled and crushed
- 2.5 cm/1 inch chunk fresh ginger, peeled, sliced and shredded
- 1 tbsp soy sauce
- ½ tbsp sesame oil
- 4 tbsp dry sherry
- 4 dried Chinese mushrooms, pre-soaked until tender, or 4 large fresh shiitake mushrooms
- 2 stalks lemon grass, or ½ tsp ground anise or five-spice powder

Place the pork in a dish having trimmed off any fat or sinews. Mix the garlic, ginger, soy, sesame oil and sherry, and pour it over the meat. Cover and refrigerate and leave for at least 2 hours or overnight, if you wish. Turn the meat in the marinade occasionally. When ready to cook the meat, remove it from the marinade, which you keep. Dry the meat, and place it in a roasting bag, together with the mushrooms and the flavouring. Close the bag and slit it in one or two places (the top half only so that the cooking juices do not run out). Place the bag in a roasting pan and cook the meat for just about an hour, at 170°C/325°F, gas mark 3. When done, carefully pour off the cooking juices into a saucepan, add the marinade, bring to the boil, reduce a little, strain and serve with the meat, carved into thin slices, with the knife held at an angle. You can, if you wish, slice the mushrooms into thin slivers before serving with the meat.

PORK STEAK TAGALOG

This recipe is based on the traditional Filipino beef steak tagalog, a simple dish of meat, marinated first and then pan-fried. It is usually served with garlic rice and a refreshing papaya chutney. It is also very good as a weekday meal served with mashed potatoes. When I was working in the kitchen at the Manila Peninsula a couple of the chefs developed a version of the recipe using thick, juicy veal steaks and chanterelles. I recommend that for a special occasion.

Serves 4

455 g/1 lb pork tenderloin,
   sliced about 1 cm/^{1}/$_2$ inch thick
2 onions, peeled and thinly sliced
2-3 tbsp soy sauce
3 tbsp fresh lime juice
1 tbsp soft brown sugar
● black pepper
1-2 tbsp corn oil or groundnut oil

Trim any fat and gristle from the pork steaks, and place in a shallow dish with a few pieces of onion in the bottom. Mix the soy sauce and lime juice with the sugar and a good pinch of black pepper, and pour over the meat. Scatter a few more pieces of onion on top and let it marinate for an hour or so, turning once or twice. Heat the oil in a fryingpan, and remove the meat from the marinade, letting the juices drip back into the dish. Fry the pork with the remaining onion until done to your liking. Remove the meat and onions from the pan, and keep them warm. Pour the marinade and marinated onions into the fryingpan, and stir up any caramelized residue

on the bottom of the pan. Add 2-3 tablespoons of water, and bring to the boil. Sieve and serve the sauce poured over the pork and onions. Cook beef steak tagalog in the same way.

BRAISED SWEET AND SOUR PIG'S TROTTERS

I find most meats too delicate for the brutal sweet and sour treatment they are sometimes given, particularly when combined with a coarse heavy batter. Here, though, the two flavours provide a perfect foil for the distinctive texture of slowly cooked pig's trotters. It makes an inexpensive, yet very tasty dish. Have the pig's trotters split down the middle and then chopped across two or three times, giving you 6-8 pieces.

Serves 4-6

4 pig's trotters
1 tbsp groundnut oil
1 medium onion, peeled and sliced
3-4 cloves garlic, peeled and crushed
140 ml/5 fl oz rice or coconut vinegar
140 g/5 fl oz light or dark muscovado sugar
2.5 cm/1 inch piece peeled ginger
1 tsp ground Szechuan pepper
4 tbsp soy sauce
3 tbsp Shaoxing wine or dry Oloroso or
   Amontillado sherry
4 spring onions or a few garlic chives
● fresh flat-leaf parsley

Fry the pig's trotters in the oil, in a heavy saucepan or casserole until browned all over. Add the onions and garlic and cook until the onion is just beginning to brown. Add the vinegar and sugar. Slice and shred the ginger and add with the pepper and soy sauce. Stir, cooking gently, until the sugar has dissolved. Pour on enough water to cover the pig's trotters, bring to the boil, boil for 3 minutes, cover, then lower the heat to a simmer or put in a low oven and cook for 3 hours, topping up with water if necessary. Half an hour before the end, add the wine and spring onions or chives, cut into shreds or lengths. Serve very hot, decorated with a few fresh parsley leaves. This is good served with a sharp green vegetable such as spinach or bok choy, or with something crunchy, such as celery or mangetouts.

BRAISED PIG'S TROTTERS AND MUSHROOMS With BLACK BEANS

This rich sticky slow-cooked dish will more or less look after itself in the oven. You can cook it for even longer in a slower oven and thus have a warming dish to come back to on a cold day. By the time they are cooked, the pig's trotters will have collapsed into tender morsels. Try serving this with a dish of stir-fried or steamed gai laan (mustard greens) flavoured with sesame oil and rice vinegar, as this makes a marvellous sharp contrast.

Serves 4

60 g/2 oz dried mushrooms
 – the best you can afford
4 pig's trotters
2 onions
2 sticks celery
2 leeks
4 cloves garlic
30 g/1 oz fermented black beans
1 bouquet garni
300 ml/10 fl oz stock, or a mixture
 of rice wine and water
● freshly ground black pepper
½ tsp five-spice powder
110 g/4 oz fresh shiitake
 or oyster mushrooms
110 g/4 oz button or cap mushrooms

Soak the dried mushrooms in water for 30-60 minutes.

Soak a clay pot in cold water for 15 minutes. Wash and dry the pig's trotters and lay these in the bottom of the casserole. Drain and trim the mushrooms and tuck them around the pig's trotters. Peel and thinly slice the vegetables and lay them on top. Add the beans, bouquet garni, the stock or wine mixture, and the pepper and spices.

Cook for 3 hours at 170°C/325°F, gas mark 3. After 2 hours, add the fresh mushrooms. Before serving you might like to strain off most of the juice, reduce it by half, season to taste and return it to the pot.

CUCUMBER AND SPARE RIBS

This is home-style cooking and not at all the sort of dish you would find in a restaurant. If you do not have a Chinese shop nearby to sell you hairy cucumbers, use courgettes or ordinary cucumbers. Cooked cucumbers are very good, provided they are not overdone.

Serves 4

8 dried Chinese mushrooms or 12 fresh
   shiitake mushrooms
6 medium-sized courgettes or 2 large
   cucumbers
570 g/1¼ lb pork spare rib chops
1 tbsp groundnut oil
● sea salt, black pepper

Soak the dried mushrooms in 5 fl oz/140 ml water for half an hour. If using fresh mushrooms poach them for 5 minutes in the same quantity of water. Drain and reserve the liquid. Slice the mushrooms. Peel the cucumber or courgettes and cut into wedges (hairy cucumbers need scraping not peeling). Dice the belly pork. Heat the oil in a wok or large fryingpan and fry the pork until browned all over. Then add the vegetables. Cook for a couple of minutes and then add half the mushroom liquid. Cook for a further minute or two, season with sea salt and freshly ground black pepper and serve immediately.

LAMB SHANKS With BRAISED CHINESE MUSHROOMS AND HARICOT BEANS

I first began to work on this idea with pork in mind. Pork and mushrooms is perhaps a more usual combination, and indeed, this recipe works well enough with knuckles of pork. It does, however, produce a very rich dish. I rather prefer the more distinct flavours and textures of the less fatty lamb. Prepare the beans the day before required by covering them with plenty of boiling water and allowing them to soak overnight. If you have no five-spice powder, use ground aniseed or cumin.

Serves 4

8-12 Chinese mushrooms
340 g/12 oz (soaked weight)
   pre-soaked beans
1 large onion
1 tbsp groundnut, sunflower
   or soya oil
4 lamb shanks
1 tsp five-spice powder
1 tsp freshly ground black pepper
1 tbsp rice vinegar
2 tbsp rice wine
● piece of tangerine peel
300 ml/10 fl oz stock or water

Soak the mushrooms in water for 30 minutes. Drain the beans. Peel and thinly slice the onion and fry until golden in the oil. Meanwhile season the meat with the spices and pepper. Fry the lamb shanks with the onion until browned all over. Sprinkle on the rice vinegar and the wine. Add the beans, tangerine peel and the water.

Bring to the boil, add the soaked mushrooms, cover and simmer very gently or cook in a low oven until the beans, mushrooms and lamb are tender, about 1½-2 hours. Check from time to time and add more water as the beans may absorb more than that added at the beginning. If you have used an oven-to-table casserole this rustic, warming dish can be served straight from the pot. A crisp salad will follow this very well.

FILLET OF SPRING LAMB
With GINGER AND CORIANDER

Serve this flavoursome dish with quickly stir-fried vegetables such as bean sprouts, shredded Chinese leaves, spinach, celery and mushrooms. Although not often found in oriental cooking, lamb lends itself very well to oriental flavours.

Serves 3-4

455 g/1 lb lamb fillet
2.5 cm/1 inch piece of fresh ginger
2 cloves garlic
3 spring onions
4 tbsp dry sherry or rice wine
1 tbsp sherry vinegar or rice vinegar
2 tsp sesame oil
2 tsp soy sauce
1 tsp crushed coriander seeds
1 tbsp groundnut or sunflower oil
• salt, pepper
• fresh coriander leaves for garnish

Trim all fat and sinews from the lamb and slice into diagonal slices for quick cooking, no more than 5 mm/¼ inch thick. Peel the ginger, garlic and spring onions. Slice the ginger into thin strips, crush the garlic and thinly slice the spring onions. Mix the wine, vinegar, sesame oil, soy sauce and coriander, stir in the ginger, garlic and spring onion and pour over the lamb fillet. Marinate overnight or at least 8 hours.

When ready to cook, pick out the meat, and dry it on paper towels, reserving the marinade. Heat the groundnut or sunflower oil in a large fryingpan or wok and when just smoking put in the lamb. Stir until browned all over and cooked the way you like it – if rare only 2-3 minutes, if well done, then 5 minutes or so. Remove the meat and keep it warm on a serving plate. Pour the marinade including the vegetables into the hot pan and reduce it until syrupy. Season to taste, strain it over the meat, garnish with coriander leaves and serve immediately with the vegetables.

LAMB VAGABOND KING

One of the famous banquet dishes of Chinese cooking is Beggar's Chicken, a highly flavoured stuffed chicken which is wrapped in first lotus leaves, then cellophane and then mud, which hardens as the chicken bakes. It is brought to the table where the host ceremonially cracks the mud and serves the tender and aromatic meat to his guests.

At the elegant Hunan Restaurant in the Taipei Hilton we were served, during the course of a meal which included shark's fin with crab roe, smoked pomfret Hunan-style and steamed beef brisket soup with yellow fungi, an interesting adaptation. It was described as "Lamb à la Vagabond King". The vagabond king referred to was supposedly the first emperor of the Han dynasty. At the suggestion of chef Ng Lin, who cooks the more authentic version at the Eagles' Nest restaurant in the Hong Kong Hilton, I have used a flour and water dough instead of mud.

You can, of course, adapt this recipe again to create the Beggar's Chicken.

Serves 6-8

1 boned leg of lamb, 1.06 kg/3½ lb, from the knuckle end
- salt
1 tsp dark soy sauce
2 tsp rice wine or Amontillado sherry
2 tsp groundnut or sunflower oil
30 g/1 oz shredded fresh ginger
4 spring onions, finely chopped
6 dried Chinese mushrooms
110 g/4 oz lean pork, cut into matchsticks
85 g/3 oz Chinese pickled cabbage, chopped
1 medium onion, peeled and chopped
1 tbsp light soy sauce
- freshly ground black pepper
1 tsp ground star anise or five-spice powder
5-6 lotus leaves, soaked in hot water until pliable
455-680 g/1-1½ lb flour

Remove the outer fat and skin from the lamb, together with any bits of gristle and open out the joint. Rub the meat lightly all over with salt. Mix the dark soy sauce, the wine, half the oil, a little shredded ginger and the spring onions, and spread this all over the lamb and marinate for an hour. Soak the mushrooms in warm water for 30 minutes, and then shred them finely, discarding the tough stalk end. Fry the pork in the remaining oil until crisp, and add the cabbage, mushrooms, onion and remaining ginger, light soy sauce, pepper and half the anise. Stir the mixture over moderate heat for 3-4 minutes. Drain off any excess oil, and heap the mixture in the centre of the opened-out leg of lamb. Wrap the meat tightly in the drained lotus leaves, sprinkling the remaining powdered anise between the leaves. Tie with string if necessary. Then put the parcel in a roasting bag or cellophane paper to ensure that all the juices are retained. Finally, add enough water to the flour to make a stiff dough and cover the parcel with it completely. Place on a baking tray, and bake in the centre of a very hot oven, 230°C/450°F, gas mark 8, for 3 hours.

To serve, crack open the dough case, and cut through the paper and leaves. The meat will be tender enough to pick up with chopsticks.

MARINATED FILLET OF BEEF

This is a delicious way of cooking the thin tail end of fillet you will get on a whole piece. Too thin to roast, it lends itself to quick cooking and oriental flavours to serve as part of a Chinese-style meat or as a warm beef salad. Occasionally butchers will sell tail end of fillet quite cheaply.

Serves 2-3

455 g/1 lb tail end of fillet
2 tbsp clear honey
2 tbsp rice or sherry vinegar,
  or lemon juice
1 tbsp soy sauce
1 tsp Angostura bitters
3 cloves garlic, peeled and crushed
3 spring onions or 1 leek, trimmed,
  washed and thinly sliced
2.5 cm/1 inch chunk of fresh ginger,
  finely chopped
1/2 tsp ground coriander
1/2 tsp five-spice powder or
  ground anise, optional

Trim fat and sinews from the meat and put it in a bowl. Combine the rest of the ingredients, pour over the meat, cover and let it marinate overnight in the refrigerator.

When ready to cook the meat, slowly heat a heavy iron fryingpan to very hot. Remove the meat from the marinade and dry it thoroughly. If there is the slightest chance that the meat will stick, very lightly oil the base of the pan before placing the meat in it. Press the meat well down with a wooden spoon or spatula and fry for 5 minutes, turn over and fry for a further 3 or 4 minutes. Remove the meat from the pan, and keep it warm while you boil up the strained marinade to make a syrupy sauce. Slice the meat thinly and obliquely, with a sharp knife held almost parallel to the top surface of the meat. Serve with the sauce poured over it.

Overleaf: Marinated Fillet of Beef

ORANGE AND LEMON BRAISED VEAL SHANKS

Veal is not a meat eaten in the Far East except in Western restaurants in the grand hotels. Because of its delicate flavour and texture, some would say its blandness, it lends itself well to spices and herbs. This recipe uses the same veal shanks, sawn across the bone, that are used to make osso bucco.

Serves 6

6 pieces of veal shank,
    about 170-225 g/6-8 oz each
30 g/1 oz seasoned flour
1 tbsp olive oil
2 celery stalks
2 shallots
2 or 3 pieces dried orange peel
2 lemon grass shoots,
    sliced into 2 or 3
1 cinnamon stick
• several sprigs fresh coriander
75 ml/3 fl oz veal or chicken
    stock, or water
2 tbsp saké or fino sherry
2 tsp soy sauce

Toss the veal in seasoned flour and fry it in the olive oil until light brown on both sides. Meanwhile trim and slice the celery stalk, and peel and slice the shallots. Lay the vegetables in the bottom of a casserole. Place the browned pieces of veal on top. Tuck the peel, lemon grass and cinnamon in between the pieces of meat. Finely chop a few of the coriander leaves and scatter on top. Deglaze the fryingpan with stock and wine, mix in the soy sauce and pour it over the veal. Cover and cook at 170°C/325°F, gas mark 3 for 2-2½ hours until the meat is falling off the bone. Serve either from the casserole or transfer the meat and vegetables to a serving dish with the cooking juices poured over it, taking care not to lose any marrow from the centre of the hollow shin bones. Decorate with the remaining fresh coriander leaves. This is very good with a plain vegetable dish, such as the Chinese leaves and mangetouts on p. 154.

BRAISED BEEF
AND
BLACK BEAN STEW

This is even better the next day, like so many casseroles. The best cut of beef to use is shin. When cooked long and slowly, it becomes tender and silky, as the gristly connective tissues break down to produce rich gravy. You can use black soya beans, black kidney beans or black turtle beans. The skins of black and red beans contain toxins which cause discomfort to some people. They are destroyed by boiling vigorously for 10-15 minutes. Then rinse the beans and soak them. Turtle beans and kidney beans could do with 4-5 hours' soaking. With the tougher soya beans it is usually easiest to soak them overnight.

Serves 6

900 g/2 lb shin beef
30 g/1 oz flour
1/2 tsp five-spice powder
1/2 tsp freshly ground black pepper
1/4 tsp ground Szechuan pepper
3 tbsp groundnut oil
1 onion
2 tbsp soaked chopped fermented
   black beans
450 ml/15 fl oz beef
   or vegetable stock
225 g/8 oz pre-soaked black beans,
   prepared as above
225 g/8 oz carrots
4 tbsp Shaoxing wine or
   dry Oloroso sherry
4 sprigs fresh coriander
2 tbsp fresh coriander leaves

Trim excess fat from the meat and cut into 2.5-5 cm/1-2 inch cubes. Put the flour and spices in a paper bag and toss the meat in it, a few chunks at a time. Fry the meat in the groundnut oil until brown all over, remove with a slotted spoon and put to one side while you fry the onion until golden brown. Stir in the fermented black beans and cook for 2-3 minutes. Moisten with a little of the stock and scrape up any cooking residues stuck to the pan. Put the meat back in the pan, together with the soaked beans and stock. Bring to the boil, cover and simmer on a very low heat or in the bottom of a moderate oven for 2-2½ hours, topping up with water or stock if the beans show signs of absorbing too much. Peel and slice the carrots, add to the stew together with the wine and sprigs of coriander. Bring to the boil and cook gently for another hour. Remove the sprigs of coriander, stir in the fresh herbs and serve.

Overleaf: Braised Beef and Black Bean Stew

STUFFED PANCAKES AND DIPPING SAUCES

Lumpia and popiah are, respectively, the Filipino and Nonya versions of Chinese spring rolls. For me they make another of those excellent DIY dishes for entertaining in a casual style, like the "dip-dip" on p. 137. The pancakes require much preparation on the part of the cook but this can be done well in advance.

Make the pancakes according to the recipe on p. 66. The garlic chives can be left out if you prefer. Triple quantities should be enough for 8 people. Use some or all of the dipping sauces described on p. 140, and in addition prepare the following accompaniments.

A SMALL DISH OF HOISIN SAUCE

This is a rich, dark, fruity sauce which you can buy bottled in oriental stores.

A SMALL DISH OF CHILLI SAUCE

2 tbsp tomato purée

2 tbsp water

1 tsp soy sauce

1 tsp toasted sesame oil

1 or 2 finely chopped, seeded chillies

Mix all ingredients together.

PORK AND PRAWN STUFFING

1 onion
1 carrot
1 celery stalk
6 water chestnuts or
a Jerusalem artichoke
170 g/6 oz lean pork tenderloin
170 g/6 oz peeled raw prawns
2 tbsp groundnut oil
1-2 tbsp soy sauce
1 tbsp sesame oil
1-2 cloves crushed garlic
● *pinch Sezchuan pepper*

Peel and roughly chop the vegetables. Dice the pork and put in a food processor with the prawns and half the vegetables; process until it has the texture of fine mince. Chop the rest of the vegetables by hand, quite finely. Mix with the pork and prawns and fry in the groundnut oil for 10-15 minutes. Season with the rest of the ingredients and pile in a bowl.

FILLINGS

● *peeled cucumber, cut in half, seeded and cut into thin slices or julienne*
● *shredded or sliced spring onions*
● *chopped coriander leaves*
● *shredded basil leaves*
● *finely sliced celery*
● *blanched chopped bean sprouts*
● *slivers of cooked ham*
● *shredded chicken*
● *shredded or grated ginger mixed with salt*

To assemble the pancakes, which is very similar to the way one tackles Peking Duck, spread on a little hoisin sauce and a dab of chilli sauce, spoon on some pork and prawn mixture then sprinkle on one or two of the other ingredients. Roll up the pancakes, turning in both ends to close them and eat after dipping in one of the dipping sauces. These rolls can also be deep-fried.

Overleaf: Stuffed Pancakes

DIP-DIPS

DIP-DIPS, HOTPOTS AND STEAM-BOATS

For informal entertaining there is nothing nicer than sitting round a table and letting everyone cook their own food in a bubbling, steaming, fragrant pot. I much prefer the oriental style using a well-flavoured stock rather than the western fondue, dipping meat into boiling oil.

Mongolian hotpot, steam-boat and "dip-dip" are some of the names you will come across all over Southeast Asia to describe essentially the same dish. I give my version below, a mixture of meats, fish and vegetables. The beauty of such an informal dish is that it can be adapted to seasonal variations and personal taste. It would be a simple matter, for example, to create a "dip-dip" for vegetarians. On the other hand, because guests choose and cook their own morsels,

all tastes can be accommodated around a single table.

There is another variation on this theme, called the Mongolian barbecue, but it is more suited to the hotel environment since you need a very large wok, griddle or paella pan and someone cooking all the time. Only one portion can be cooked at a time. It is fun, though, to make a selection from the large variety of neatly sliced meats, vegetables, herbs, spices, and condiments which you arrange on top of a pile of rice and hand to the cook, who tosses the mixture on the sizzling surface and stir fries it for you. But, back to the "dip-dip", which is the Malaysian name for this charming custom (called *da bin lo* in Chinese).

ORIENTAL DIP-DIP

Serves 8-10

MEATS

*225 g/8 oz fillet steak (can be taken
    from the less expensive tail end)*
225 g/8 oz pork tenderloin
225 g/8 oz lamb fillet
*225 g/8 oz skinless chicken breast or
    12 chicken wings*

Firm up the meat fillets by putting in the freezer
or ice-making compartment of the refrigerator,
well wrapped, for an hour. With a very sharp
knife, slice into paper thin slices (or as close to
that as you can get) and arrange each meat on a
separate plate in a neat pattern. If using chicken
wings, cut off and discard the wing tip and
divide the remaining part in two at the joint.
Cover each plate of meat with cling film, stack
one on top of the other and refrigerate until
required.

FISH

- *prawn balls*
- *fish balls*
- *uncooked prawns*
- *fresh scallops or queen scallops*

PRAWN OR FISH BALLS

*445 g/1lb raw, peeled prawns or skinless
    white fish fillet*
2-3 tsp cornflour

*2 spring onions, trimmed and finely
    chopped or 4 garlic chives, finely
    chopped*
*1 tsp finely grated orange zest or
    dried peel (for the fish balls)*
1 lightly beaten egg white

Put the prawns or fish in the food processor
with 2 teaspoons cornflour and process until
smooth. Mix in the spring onions or chives, and
the orange peel if using it. Stir in the egg white
and more cornflour if necessary to bind the
mixture, which should be firm enough to
handle. Wet your hands and roll into walnut-
sized balls. Put on a plate, cover lightly with
cling film and refrigerate until required.

VEGETABLES

Use a selection from the following and
prepare them as appropriate to give bite-
sized pieces. Some will not need cutting up,
some will.

- *mangetouts*
- *fine green beans*
- *Chinese leaves and/or bok choy*
- *oyster mushrooms*
- *shiitake mushrooms or soaked
    mushrooms*
- *baby corn cobs*

Arrange the vegetables in bowls or on plates and
keep covered until required.

Overleaf: Dip-Dip

Noodles

455 g/1 lb thin rice or wheat noodles

Cook these as for noodle salads on p. 61, refresh, drain and put to one side until required.

Sauces

You can also use the spicy sauce on p. 46 which accompanies the chicken and coconut soup, as well as the dipping sauce on p. 60.

Chilli Vinegar

4 tbsp rice vinegar
2 tbsp water
1 tbsp sugar
1-2 chillies, finely sliced

Mix the vinegar, water and sugar, and add the chillies.

Ginger Vinegar

Prepare as above but substitute 2 table-spoons finely grated ginger for the chillies.

Garlic Vinegar

Prepare as above but substitute 2 or 3 peeled, crushed garlic cloves mixed with a little salt.

Coconut Sauce

1 small onion, peeled and thinly sliced
5-7. 5 cm/2-3 inches thick end
  of lemon grass, thinly sliced
1 tsp crushed coriander seeds
1 tbsp groundnut oil

85 g/3 oz coconut cream,
  broken off a block
3 tbsp stock

Fry the onion, lemon grass and coriander in the oil until the mixture is fragrant. Stir in the coconut cream and when it has melted, add enough stock to give the sauce a good consistency for dipping.

Stock

2.3 l/4 pints chicken or vegetable stock
1-2 tbsp chopped coriander leaves
7.5 cm/3-4 inches thin end of
  lemon grass, thinly sliced
2-3 spring onions, trimmed and finely sliced

Bring the stock to the boil and transfer it to a large casserole, fondue pot or hotpot set over a table candle or spirit burner. Food is taken up with fondue forks, chopsticks or those small mesh baskets on long handles which so resemble fishing nets, and held in the simmering stock until cooked, when it is transferred to the individual bowl or plate, being dipped into a sauce en route, and then eaten. You can also thread two or three different ingredients on a long wooden skewer as they do in Malaysia and dip it into the stock to cook. The stock of course gets better and better as the dipping progresses. When all the morsels have been cooked, put the noodles in a colander and pour boiling water over them to heat through or put them in a large bowl of hot water. Drain them and divide between soup bowls, enough for each guest, and ladle the stock over the noodles.

MORE CITIES
IN
SOUTHEAST ASIA

SINGAPORE AND KUALA LUMPUR

On our first visit to Singapore in 1988, we approached it in a thoughtful mood, having left behind us Hong Kong, Shanghai, Guangzhou and Taipei. Friends who knew how much we loved Hong Kong warned us not to have very high hopes of Singapore. Sterile, ultra-modern, soulless, glass and concrete were epithets that we heard over and over again.

Changi Airport is large, well appointed, pleasant, uncrowded and efficient, and we were out of it in no time being driven to our hotel along the wide, bougainvillea and oleander-lined East Coast Parkway, with sea and dark green islands to our left, parkland and neat housing estates to our right. Very tall, slender shimmering skyscrapers beckoned from the hazy distance. It all seemed clean, tidy and efficient after Taipei. What's wrong with a tropical, oriental Switzerland, we wondered?

That first evening in a new place is always exciting. We were being so well looked after that it was hard to tear ourselves away from our comfortable rooms with their glorious views over the harbour, the city, the islands and the newly reclaimed Marina area. Singapore is packed with fine hotels: the Regent, the Hilton, the Meridien in the Orchard Road shopping area, and then the new ones down in Marina Square designed by John Portman, he of the soaring, plant-swathed atria and glass lifts. That is where we were staying, at the Oriental. Luscious tropical fruits, orchids and champagne, the glorious pool, its excellent restaurants, all conspired to keep us there but in the end we stepped out of the air-conditioned coolness to a soft blue evening whose warmth and humidity hung around us like a velvet curtain.

We walked to Raffles and had beers in the Writers Bar. It is a wonderful old hotel, with cool floors, overhead fans, colonnades and balconies, trees and rickshaws. All this atmosphere made it possible to overlook the coachloads of tourists arriving for the evening's cultural show, and the ready-made Singapore Slings lined up four deep on all the bars. We sat for a long while over our drinks thinking about the travellers and writers who had been there before us. Then inevitably thoughts turned to dinner. It was either back to the hotel for enticing Asian dishes at the Café Palm, or out into the streets to follow our noses. We chose to explore, and so came to the Satay Centre and the Esplanade Food Centre. Having heard that the hawkers' stalls set up at the roadside from a bicycle or cart had been made illegal, and that the hawkers were now gathered together in "centres", we had imagined something rather cheerless and unappealing. Not a bit of it. Here were stalls of all descriptions, lit by bright lights advertising their specialities, and stallholders beckoning us over to have a look. Most tables in the centre were full, but others soon became free and so we sat down once we had chosen our meal from the exuberant and exotic array of specialities.

Exuberant is a word that often comes to mind when I try to describe Singaporean and Malaysian food. It is just the kind of food I like; fresh ingredients prepared by skilled cooks who produce dishes full of good smells. You could do much worse in Singapore than eat all your meals in such places. Do not be put off by the bustle and the hawkers shouting their wares – walk round and take your time choosing, then go and sit at any of the tables and your food will be brought to you. This and places like it are where Singaporeans like to eat and to bring their friends. In earlier years, hawking dishes of their own food from bicycles was the sole source of income for many immigrants. Gradually the stands were centralized and hygiene standards were imposed and continue to be maintained by government health inspectors. Standards are high, prices are fair and competitive.

What a profusion of smells and flavours we experienced that night and what a variety of people we saw. Muslims in skull caps and long robes fanned small grills with palm leaf fans to cook lamb, beef and chicken satay sticks to a juicy tenderness with a crisp, charcoaled coating. These were served with a fiery chilli and peanut sauce. Chinese cooks in shorts and sandals were grilling tiger prawns and others were ladling out platefuls of guo tiao (kway teow), the broad, flat noodles that are first cooked then stir-fried with a mixture of prawns, pork and bean sprouts. Mee rebus and chee fan are also dishes to look for on the hawker stalls; the first is noodles with beef, prawns and beans and in a thick brown chilli sauce; the second, slices of chicken served with rice cooked in chicken stock and flavoured with ginger and chillies, somewhat like the Hainanese chicken dish. We could also have feasted on Indian curries and paratha, Thai specialities, Malay roti john, pork rib soup, or barbecued fish. All were to be had for just a few Singapore dollars and could be washed down with Tiger beer, or better still, coconut juice. I never tired of this. Coconuts with the outer green husk carved off were piled up in glass-fronted refrigerated counters. The top is sliced off in front of you, and you are given a straw to suck out the cool sweet juice and a long-handled spoon with which to scoop out the thin layer of soft, jelly-like flesh, which is a perfect ending to a meal.

This great delicacy is something that will be permanently associated with our visits to Singapore. It was something to be looked forward to after a long dusty walk down Beach Road. This is one of the older, unrenovated parts of the city. "Shop-houses" which are just what their names suggest, houses on top and shops beneath, line the street, and shaded colonnades protect you from the worst of the sun. The open fronts display all manner of business enterprises, printing shops, small canteens and restaurants, a shop selling fishing tackle, the irresistible Dustager Bros selling spices from huge sacks on the floor. Imagine digging your hands into a deep hessian sack full of star anise pods. We bought some of these, together with cardamom pods, and cinnamon sticks, which were tied together in bundles two feet long. I still have a few perfumed sticks left which are so sweet and fragrant that I like to break off a piece and just chew on it. At Joo Hiang Private Ltd we watched tea being carefully weighed and packaged. We came away having bought tiny half-ounce parcels of the dark strong ti kwan yin tea wrapped in paper printed with a colour picture of the Iron Goddess of Mercy herself.

We visited the wet market known locally as KK Market at the beginning of Little India, but walked first down Serangoon Road, peering into restaurants and gold shops and visiting the beautiful temple with the steeply pitched roof crowded with carved and painted figures like a grandstand on Ladies' Day. The market was a large open high-roofed hall. Leading into it from the entrance are the food stalls, where you can buy wonderful take-aways, or where you can sit down and eat your Singapore noodles or beef rendang. The Chinese stalls are down one side, the Malay stalls down the other. The larger part of the market is the produce section, which has a profusion of scented flowers and leaves as well as piles of glossy fruit and fresh leaf vegetables. This is where Singaporeans shop. It is like good markets everywhere. People are not rude but they push and jostle because they are in a hurry. Stallholders are brisk and waste no time because they have other customers to serve. It is all very good-humoured. I'm sure if we lived in Singapore we would make daily visits there. As it was I was terribly tempted to buy some of the wet spice mixtures which are ground and mixed for you in the proportions and combinations you require to produce velvety smooth and hot beef rendang and the tangy Nonya curry rich with coconut cream.

All this makes one very hungry. We set off to find some Nonya food. When the original Chinese settlers crossed the Straits of Malacca to peninsular Malaya from the rural districts of Swatow, Hainan and Hokkien, they brought few women with them and so married into the indigenous Malay Muslim population. The unique hybrid culture that developed is known as Peranakan or Straits Chinese, and its food is known as Nonya, after the women who cook it (Peranakan men are known as Babas). It blends the original peasant Chinese dishes with spicy Malay food to produce such dishes as chap chye lemak and buah keluak ayam in a now classic form of cooking.

In Holland Village, we were told, we would find a very good Peranakan restaurant. Holland Village is a charming area. Behind the well-stocked Cold Storage Supermarket in Holland Avenue we found more food stalls, cafés, a wine bar called Palms, shops selling rattan and basketwork and other pretty shop-houses. But no Peranakan restaurant. We noticed some serious-looking civil servants going into Hsieh's Garden and followed them. Our curiosity was well rewarded. The lady who was cooking said it was a Cantonese restaurant but it was certainly not like any Cantonese food we had tasted in Hong Kong or in Guangzhou. We learned that the cook had been born in Singapore and had never been anywhere else. Her cooking had a wonderful and subtle spiciness and sweetness that sums up Singaporean food for me. The paper-wrapped chicken was brilliant. Small joints had been marinated for a day in ginger, honey, spring onion, salt and pepper (at least, that's what I guessed, for she would not part with any secrets). Each piece was then wrapped in a parcel of greaseproof paper and deep-fried until done. The recipe on p. 100 is as close as I can get. We also ate Hainanese pork chops, fish dipped in seasoned flour and then stir-fried, and delicious noodles with pork, bean sprouts and sesame seeds. We drank beer with our lunch. We could also have tried sotong ball (cuttlefish), chilli crabs, clay pot lobster and roast pigeon. Apart from the civil servants and post office workers, the other diners were local housewives with their children. Hsieh's Garden is very basic with plastic tabletops and plastic plates and spoons. It is at 15A Lorong Liput, and is an experience not to be missed.

Nonya food will be found at Bibi's Nonya Restaurant in Peranakan Place at 180 Orchard Road. More than a restaurant, this is a showcase for the Peranakan culture. You can find various handicrafts there as well as watch a re-enactment of a Peranakan wedding. In the Katong District around Joo Chiat Road you will also find restaurants serving Nonya food, such as the Guan Hoe Soon. In fact, you scarcely need a guide to where to eat in Singapore. There are so many good restaurants, at all levels, offering every imaginable type of food, that you need only follow your nose. And you will, in that way, make exciting discoveries which are yours alone. One of the finest Thai meals we've ever eaten was at a very simple little restaurant in the basement of a soulless shopping centre called Centrepoint on Orchard Road. The restaurant was called The Parkway and we chose chicken pandan (small pieces of chicken wrapped in fragrant pandanus leaves and fried), tom yam goulay (a spicy, hot and sour fish soup) satay, fried glass noodles, barbecued cuttlefish and a really delicious fish "custard", steamed in banana leaf cups, and flavoured with shallots, lemon grass, coconut and only a little chilli.

You may also sample fine European cooking in Singapore. Maxims de Paris is in the Regent of Singapore. It serves utterly authentic, exquisite French food. And last time we were in Singapore, Louis Outhier cooked dinner for us at Restaurant La France in Le Meridien just behind Orchard Road.

One morning on our last visit to Singapore, we went to Cuppage Centre, one of those places that look more like a three- or four-storey car park but which houses on the ground floor fish and meat stalls, all gleaming and fresh, on the first floor a rich profusion of fruit and vegetables, and on the top floor a "food centre". Even at 10.30 in the morning, it was full of business people, market people, shop girls, clerks, schoolgirls and housewives, all eating everything that Singapore has to offer from turtle soup to cendol, nasi lemak to laksa, chicken rice to roti john.

After all those hunger-making smells, we decided to go back to Hsieh's Garden, which we had discovered on our first visit two years earlier. Again we walked around the delightful area of Holland Village, along Lorong Liput and Lorong Mambong, as well as through the small wet market. We saw eating houses, coffee houses (kopi tiam), restaurants, even El Felipe's Cantina, an authentic-looking Mexican restaurant. Shops selling cane ware and other furniture, hats and walking sticks, pots and porcelain make this a good place for souvenir-hunting. But it is a residential area, not a tourist haunt, and all the more pleasant for it. The Cold Storage would be a good place to stock up on spices and herbs to take back home – makrut leaves, limau kesturi (the tiny limes or calamansi), the knobbly green fragrant limes used in Thai cooking, lemon grass, pandanus leaves, and the strange hard nut, buah kelak. Bags of spices for making the famous pork ribs tea or bah kut tee, rendang spices, Nonya curry and fish-head curry spices also make good presents. Small flower shops sell orchids at a fraction of the price you will pay at the airport or lobby shops of the grand hotels.

In the window of Hsieh's Garden was a copy of a review I had written for a magazine two years previously. And the restaurant was closed. It was a Tuesday. I should have re-read my notes before we left London. However, we found the Nonya restaurant we had looked for on our first visit. It is called Oleh Sayang and is both charming and simple. You feel you are eating in someone's home. A few dishes are cooked at lunch-time, family-style, and you point to what you want. The Nonya chicken churry and chicken korma were both delicious as was the chop choy or chap chye, Nonya-style braised mixed cabbages with mushrooms. Sago honeydew was a lovely soothing dessert, sago cooked in coconut milk and mixed with shreds of melon. Fresh lime juice and homemade barley water completed our meal.

For an evening of feasting, try somewhere like Mosque Street off New Bridge Road. The area is full of stalls, restaurants and kopi tiam (a mixed Malay and Chinese phrase which means coffee house). Here you will find one of my favourite dishes, the Hakka yong tau foo or stuffed bean curd. Sometimes it is made from both the soft white and the firmer deep-fried bean curd, and bean curd skins; sometimes it is more elaborate and includes stuffed chillies, okra and brinjal (aubergines), all in a flavoursome bowl of broth. The filling is a mixture of minced fish, minced dried cuttlefish and minced pork. Save one evening too for the kopi tiam along Geylong Road and the various lorongs (streets or lanes) running off it. I went there one evening with Violet Oon, Singapore's leading food expert and a fine cook herself. We first went for Chinese satay in the kopi tiam on the corner of Geylong Road and Lorong 9 at 549, beneath the Yew Lian Hotel. See Hock Siong has a stall in the same kopi tiam, where his speciality is fried Hokkien mee (noodles). This will remain in my memory as probably the best dish I have eaten in Singapore. It was rich in pork stock and lard and had huge prawns and fried egg all bound together by the wheaty, succulent noodles. Apparently this version is so good because of the real "wok" flavour of charcoal.

Further along Geylong, we passed a tiny mosque and a Chinese temple, side by side, as well as lovely old tile-fronted shop-houses. It is far from the truth to say that "all" of Singapore has been pulled down to make way for the new. This eastern part of the city has a delightful between-the-wars feel to it. Two-storey, pastel coloured houses have colonnaded fronts with tiled patios and shutters on the upstairs windows; orange trees, bougainvilleas and hibiscus stand in pots on the patios. Frangipani and oleander trees line the streets, mingling their fragrance with the heady smells of charcoal-fired wok burners, barbecuing prawns and frying noodles. Even though it was well after midnight when we sat down outside the Keat Seng Coffee Shop on the corner of Geylong and Lorong 29 there was plenty of street life: families, groups of friends and "gangs", all sitting around chatting, eating and gesticulating. The atmosphere was thoroughly good-natured. Here a group of fierce-looking Cantonese ladies cooked "hor fun" for us, a marvellous tender beef dish with broad noodles and a delicious gravy, steamed fish and sweet-and-sour pork. The opening hours are every day from 7 p.m. until the food runs out in the early hours of the morning. It is hard to imagine food ever running out in Singapore. It's what makes the city tick.

I still have a number of things on my itinerary for future visits to Singapore. I want to spend more time in Chinatown and visit some of the temples as well as the bird-singing concert. I want to visit the hydroponic mushroom farm and the orchid farm, although I think I can give the alligator farm a miss. The botanical gardens and the Jurong Bird Park are quiet oases of calm if you want to get away from shopping and eating.

In 1989 we paid our first visit to Malaysia. We flew to Kuala Lumpur's Subang airport over rubber plantations. We could see the Highlands in the distance and imagined the tea plantations and old colonial houses. Our first and lasting impression of the city was one of charm, dignity, space and greenness. Car drivers seemed to follow the rules of the road which made walking the streets not too hazardous. Humidity, heat and jet-lag conspired against us, however.

Markets were first on our list of places to visit. Elizabeth Soo, the public relations director at the Hilton, disarmingly admitted that she was much too smart a lady to go to markets, but she gathered that Pudu market and Imbi Road market were the ones to go to. In the end, it was a taxi driver who persuaded us to try the Chow Kit Market, just off Jalan Tuanku Abdul Rahman, which is the main shopping street, a mixture of small shop-houses, banks and department stores.

We could smell the market as soon as we opened the taxi door. Here we were in June, the beginning of the durian season. The fruit stalls were hung with catty bunches of rambutan, some red, some yellow (a catty is a weight of about 600 g/1¼ lb), and heaped with mangosteens and brilliant pink lychees. Mangoes and long green pineapples were for sale as were coconuts, green or dry – or you could buy coconut ground to order on an impressive machine that scraped out and shredded the flesh of each coconut half. There was an abundance of fish, fresh and dried, saltwater and freshwater – tilapia, kurau, mackerel, grouper, sea bass, prawns, clams, tiny silvery pomfret and much, much more that I could not recognize. Fragrant leaves, herbs and nuts were piled high next to an assortment of chillies, long slender lilac brinjal (aubergines), silky bindi (okra), tomatoes and onions.

Back at the Planters Inn in the Hilton we tasted Malaysian food, very good satay, kway teow, nasi lemak and best of all the yong tau fu, which Elizabeth Soo translated as stuffed beancurd. In fact this splendid dish included not only cubes of beancurd and beancurd skin, but okra, chillies and brinjal, each item stuffed with cuttlefish paste and simmered in broth. It is very good indeed. Lunch turned into what is described in K.L. as high tea and we went on to try kueh, the famous Malay cake, deep-fried dates (dipped in batter first) more laksa, cuttlefish balls and spring rolls.

In Chinatown, food stalls were interspersed with those selling fake Calvin Klein, Benetton and YSL T-shirts, not to mention Ray-Ban sunglasses. Appetizing smells came from the deep-frying of breadfruit and jackfruit. We watched a cook deftly making hoppas, bowl-shaped pancakes with an egg cracked into them. You have to be even more deft to eat hoppas without getting egg yolk up to your elbows.

Central Market, which used to be the main produce market, has been turned into a handicraft and food market. This has been well done and is an excellent place to go for batik and carvings, as well as for a casual lunch. The Kampung Pandan, the city sister of a restaurant where you eat outside under the pandanus trees, is a must. It is a Muslim Indian restaurant whose most celebrated dish is the fish-head curry. This is a large dish on which reposes the head, jaws open, of a huge red snapper served in a light curry sauce, very fragrant and spicy and slightly sour with tamarind. Grilled prawns, curried prawns and beef rendang were also exceptionally good. We were offered marvellous juices to drink: yellow or red watermelon, fresh lime, pineapple, sweet mango or green mango, and star fruit, although these, like the beer, are relatively expensive when compared with food prices.

Malaysia is the home of another, very different cuisine. We had already eaten Nonya food in Singapore, and now we had another opportunity to sample this enticing blend of Chinese and Malay ingredients and techniques. To do so we went off to Malacca or Melaka, a couple of hours from Kuala Lumpur. The drive is an attractive one and you are soon out into lush green countryside, not as densely growing as you might expect of tropical rainforest. And what was utterly unexpected for me was the autumnal colouring to the trees. We were promised a look at the rubber plantations, yet we drove on and on, not a rubber tree in sight. We pulled up by the roadside and there was a tree with scored bark, a cup attached to it and in the cup a milky white substance, latex. This was a rubber tree? Expecting a large-scale version of the broad, shiny-leafed houseplant we call a rubber plant, I was unprepared for this tall, slender tree with small leaves, which change colour and fall every eighteen months. Hence the autumn colours on our drive.

We turned off the main north-south highway, which will eventually be a major trunk road linking Bangkok and Singapore, and went towards the coast.

In its heyday in the 15th century, the Sultanate of Malacca was one of the world's major spice trading centres, attracting Venetian, Portuguese, Dutch and British custom. In succeeding centuries it was colonized by whoever had the strongest and furthest-reaching navy, first the Portuguese, then the Dutch and finally the British, before Malaysia became independent in 1957. Each has left its mark on Malacca. There are the curved red gables of the Stadhuys built by the Dutch, the Porta de Santiago left by the Portuguese, and the memorial tablets in Christchurch from the days of the early British colonists. But it was the Chinese who left the most vivid legacy: their food.

In the 1400s Prince Paremeswara forged an alliance with the Emperor of China through his Emissary Admiral Ho, and eventually the Emperor sent his daughter to marry the Prince, who by then had converted to Islam. This royal marriage fused the two cultures, and paved the way for many more marriages between the two races. The Straits Chinese today are those whose ancestors came as settlers to Malacca from China and married local Malay women. Out of this union was born Nonya cooking, which is found mainly in Malacca, Penang and Singapore.

The drive back to the airport gives a chance to see some more of this delightful city on its way to school and work. Neatly dressed children with smart satchels and uniforms climb into old-fashioned yellow school buses. The roads, good roads, are full of shiny new cars with good drivers. There are plenty of mopeds but few cyclists, and traffic police seem efficient. The city is a pleasing architectural mix: there are old Chinese shop-houses, modern glass-palace hotels, some traditional Moorish and Victorian Mogul architecture such as the Law Courts, the Arabian nights style of the turreted and minareted railway station, the mock Tudor Selangor Club, soaring and inspired modern Islamic architecture and many Edwardian colonial buildings. It is a green city too. Trees line busy streets, there are parks and gardens and a flourishing mixture of English suburban tidiness and flamboyant equatorial rainforest. With only a muddy river confluence (which is the translation of Kuala Lumpur) and no sea coast or lake, Kuala Lumpur is nevertheless one of the most attractive cities I have ever visited.

It is a charming mixture of oriental endeavour and tropical sloth.

For those who find Bangkok too polluted and just too difficult to deal with, and Singapore too squeaky-clean, then Kuala Lumpur is an urban paradise. The city fathers plan to keep it that way. Old buildings must be restored rather than demolished. Gardens and parks continue to be established wherever new housing goes up. Plans are afoot to lessen the impact of traffic in the city, which means that an evening spent wandering amongst the gerais or mobile stalls, which open once the sun has set and work is finished for the day, will become, if possible, an even more agreeable pastime than it already is.

VEGETABLES

BRAISED CELERY HEARTS

This is a perfect accompaniment to slow roasts and braises, as it can cook alongside them in the oven. It is particularly good with beef and, of course, with the Christmas turkey recipe on p. 113. I have given the recipe in the right sort of quantity to accompany the turkey.

Serves 6-8

1 tbsp toasted sesame oil
4 prepared celery hearts
60 g/2 oz cured ham
4 star anise
140 ml/5 fl oz vegetable, chicken
   or turkey stock
• freshly ground black pepper or Szechuan
   pepper

Lightly brush an ovenproof dish with the sesame oil. Split the celery hearts in two or three lengthways, depending on thickness. Chop or shred the ham very finely and scatter it over the celery. Tuck the spices in between, and pour the stock over the celery. Sprinkle with pepper, cover and bake for about 1½ hours at 180°C/350°F, gas mark 4.

SOY-GLAZED TURNIPS *With* SESAME SEEDS

The peppery earthiness of the turnips, the intense savouriness of the soy sauce, and the crisp nuttiness of the sesame seeds make an excellent combination in this inexpensive vegetable dish.

Serves 4-6

455 g/1 lb small turnips or navets
1 tbsp groundnut oil
60 g/2 oz light muscovado sugar
3-4 tbsp soy sauce
2 tbsp toasted sesame seeds

Peel and slice the turnips. Put them in a heavy saucepan with the groundnut oil and cook them until halfway tender. Add the sugar and cook gently until the sugar has dissolved. Stir in the soy sauce and continue cooking until the turnips are tender. Transfer to a hot serving dish and sprinkle with sesame seeds.

NOTE Parsnips, carrots, beetroot, yams, jicama (yam bean), mooli, sweet potato and other root vegetables benefit from the same sort of treatment. Use less sugar for the sweeter vegetables, and also add a splash of rice or coconut vinegar.

GARLIC CHIVES *With* BACON

These are very good with grilled meats, particularly the more delicate ones, or a boned stuffed saddle of rabbit.

Serves 6

110 g/4 oz smoked bacon, in a piece
340 g/12 oz garlic chives
  2 tbsp rice vinegar

Cut the bacon into matchsticks and fry gently until the fat runs and the bacon crisps. It can be left to do this while you prepare the garlic chives. Wash the bundle and cut into three or four lengths for easy manoeuvrability with fork or chopsticks. Blanch them in plenty of boiling water for a minute or two, drain and place in a heated serving dish. Raise the heat under the bacon and then pour the hot bacon and fat over the greens. Deglaze the pan with vinegar and pour this on top. Mix thoroughly and serve immediately.

GLAZED CARROT CURLS *With* SHREDDED GINGER AND CORIANDER

This is an excellent way of using preserved ginger and some of its syrup.

Serves 4-6

340 g/12 oz carrots
  1 tbsp groundnut oil
  1 tbsp ginger syrup
  1 tbsp lemon juice
    or tamarind liquid
  2.5 cm/1 inch piece crystallized ginger,
    peeled and shredded
  1 tbsp chopped fresh coriander leaves

Peel the carrots and, using a potato peeler, whittle into long strips. Drop these into iced salted water, to keep them fresh and moist. Leave for 20 minutes. Drain, and fry them in the groundnut oil. Cover with a lid and let them steam in their own juices for 3 or 4 minutes. Stir in the rest of the ingredients until well blended and serve immediately.

STEAMED CHINESE LEAVES AND MANGETOUTS

Serves 6

1 head of Chinese leaves
85 g/3 oz mangetouts
2 star anise

DRESSING

2 tsp sesame oil
2 tsp soy sauce
2 tsp brown sugar
2 tsp rice vinegar

Remove any damaged outer leaves from the Chinese leaves. Top and tail the mangetouts. Shred the leaves across, mix them with the mangetouts and place them in a steamer basket with the star anise buried in the middle. Steam for 5 minutes and serve immediately.

If this is a little too plain for you, mix together the ingredients for the dressing, pour it into a serving bowl and toss the drained vegetables in it.

VEGETABLE "NOODLES"

J like the way this dish looks, like colourful wide noodles, but made of vegetables not dough. They can be steamed or stir-fried and are excellent with all kinds of other dishes, meat, fish or perhaps best of all, seafood. For a very effective and beautifully simple dish, I pile a bundle of vegetable "noodles" into a steamer basket and lay a few scallops on top. Served plain or with a dipping sauce, it's a lovely light dish.

Serves 6

2 carrots
2 courgettes
1 mooli
1 oriental radish
2 leeks

Peel all the vegetables and then, using a potato peeler, shave off long strips. Drop these into iced, lightly salted water to keep them crisp as you do the rest of the vegetables. The leeks, of course, are not dealt with in the same way but simply cut in half lengthways, and then again. Drain and cook them according to your chosen method. Before serving they can be dressed with a mixture of sesame oil, soy sauce, lime juice or rice vinegar and some chopped, soaked black beans.

WINE-BRAISED FLOWER MUSHROOMS ON SPINACH

Rather than serve this with meat or fish, it is a dish to be enjoyed in its own right and then only on a special occasion, as these mushrooms are so expensive. A version can be made using fresh shiitake mushrooms, but it will not have the same deep flavours. This recipe is based on one cooked for us by Carmel Chow, a Hong Kong friend. Dining with him is to experience a most exquisite combination of the best of Cantonese food matched with the finest French (and occasionally New World) wines. I think he cooked the dish in rice wine. Cooking it in Alsace wine works very well. These mushrooms deserve the best.

Serves 6

18-24 flower mushrooms
1.35 kg/3 lb fresh spinach
1 tbsp groundnut oil
3 cloves garlic
300 ml/10 fl oz Gewurztraminer,
Riesling or Tokay d'Alsace

Soak the mushrooms in hot water for 30 minutes and remove the stalks. Trim the spinach of any hard stalks, and blanch it in plenty of boiling water for 1 minute. Drain, run it under cold water and then dry very thoroughly between layers of kitchen paper. Oil an oven-proof dish or casserole and cover the bottom with spinach. Peel and thinly slice the garlic and lay this on the spinach. Arrange the mushrooms on top, rounded surfaces uppermost. Pour on the wine, cover and cook at 170°C/325°F, gas mark 3, in the bottom half of the oven for 1-1½ hours until the mushrooms are tender and succulent.

STIR-FRIED GINGER BRUSSELS SPROUTS

Not my favourite vegetable, but they are such a favourite with most other people that it is hard to ignore them. This recipe is based on the way Anton Mosimann used to cook them for Christmas dinner at the Dorchester. It is important to use the two types of ginger.

Serves 6-8

1.35 kg/3 lb Brussels sprouts
2 shallots
3 cloves garlic
5 cm/2 inch piece fresh ginger
5 cm/2 inch piece crystallized ginger
4 tbsp groundnut or sunflower oil
4 tbsp water
● sea salt
● white pepper

Prepare and trim the sprouts, removing any damaged outer leaves and thick stalks. Shred them finely crossways. A food processor makes very fast work of this. Peel and finely chop the shallots and garlic. Peel the fresh ginger, slice and cut into juliennes. Do the same with the crystallized ginger.

Heat the oil in a wok and add the shallots and garlic. Fry without browning them or the garlic will become bitter. Stir in the sprouts and the ginger and cook for 2-3 minutes. Add the water. Cover the pan and steam the vegetables for 2-3 minutes more, shaking the pan now and then. Season lightly and serve immediately.

DESSERTS

GINGER TEA AND GRANITA

Although little game is eaten in the Far East, a ginger tea might be drunk after just such a dish to ease the digestion and sweeten the mouth. Allowed to cool and then frozen it makes a wonderfully sharp, clear palate cleanser. Peter Knipp, formerly chef at the Shanghai Hilton, suggested palm sugar for the syrup if possible. Otherwise use granulated sugar or golden granulated.

Serves 8–10
in small cups, or 6 as a
granita

570 ml/1 pint water
280 g/10 oz sugar
  5 cm/2 inch piece ginger,
    peeled and sliced

Put the water and sugar in a saucepan and heat gently until the sugar has dissolved. Simmer gently for 3 minutes. Put in the ginger, remove from the heat and allow it to infuse for 10 minutes. Strain and serve.

  Alternatively, cool then freeze.

MANGO MOUSSE

Here is an easy mango recipe which produces a deliciously light, clean-tasting pudding.

Serves 4

2 leaves gelatine
300 ml/10 fl oz organic apple juice
110 g/4 oz silken tofu
  1 ripe, fragrant mango
  2 egg whites
• sugar, optional
• toasted flaked almonds

Soften the gelatine in a little of the apple juice. Heat 140 ml/7 fl oz apple juice and add the gelatine plus juice, stirring until completely dissolved. Put the tofu in the blender. Peel the mango, catching as much of the juice as possible in the blender, put in the fruit pulp, the gelatine mixture and the rest of the juice. Sweeten if you like. Blend until smooth. Whisk the egg whites until stiff and fold into the mango mixture. Pour into a dish, chill and set. Garnish with toasted almonds.

CUSTARD APPLE SORBET

Such rare, delicious and expensive fruit is best enjoyed on its own, but should you ever have more than you know what to do with, try this delicately flavoured sorbet.

Serves 6

110 g/4 oz sugar
110 ml/4 fl oz water
  2 custard apples
  • juice of half a lemon

Make a syrup with the sugar and water and allow it to cool. Break open the custard apples and spoon out the creamy flesh, discarding the shiny black seeds. Mix the flesh, syrup and lemon juice in a blender and freeze in an ice cream maker or sorbetière according to the manufacturer's instructions.

NOTE Mango, papaya, banana, star apple, melon, pomegranate, persimmon, pineapple and other fruits can be made into sorbets in the same way. Some will take a larger quantity of syrup than others. Experiment too with the amount of sugar you use. Much depends on the ripeness of the fruit but it is a sad fact that the best-textured sorbets do have a good deal of sugar in them. Reduce the sugar content too much and you may have a hard, grainy, icy sorbet.

COLD VANILLA AND LEMON GRASS SOUP With BERRIES

This dish, although called a soup, is served as a light and refreshing sweet course.

Serves 4-6

 60 g/2 oz ground almonds
450 ml/15 fl oz full cream milk
  1 vanilla pod
  1 piece lemon grass
  • unrefined sugar to taste
300 ml/10 fl oz single cream
340 g/12 oz mixed soft fruit as available – raspberries, loganberries, wild strawberries, red or blackcurrants

GARNISH

  • frosted redcurrants or blackcurrants and leaves

Put the ground almonds in a pudding basin. In a heavy saucepan bring the milk with the vanilla pod and lemon grass to boiling point and pour it over the ground almonds. Sweeten the mixture to taste and allow to cool. Strain the milk into another bowl or jug, pressing down on the ground almonds to extract as much flavour as possible. Stir in the single cream. Chill. Hull, trim and wash the fruit as necessary and let it drain. Arrange in four shallow soup plates and pour the vanilla cream over the fruit. Garnish with frosted fruit and leaves and serve immediately.

ALMOND BEANCURD *With* JASMINE SYRUP

This delicate and light dessert is not made from beancurd, but resembles it in texture. Chef Lo at the Shanghai Hilton serves his almond beancurd with a few spoons of crème de menthe poured over it. Not my taste, but it gives an idea of the versatility of the dish. Instead of jasmine flowers, try making a syrup flavoured with lavender or roses.

Serves 6

FOR THE SYRUP

1 tbsp jasmine tea with plenty
   of flowers in it
300 ml/10 fl oz water
170 g/6 oz sugar
2 tbsp lychee liqueur, optional

Pour boiling water over the tea leaves and infuse for 15-20 minutes. Strain into a saucepan, stir in the sugar and when it has melted, boil the syrup for 2-3 minutes. Allow it to cool and stir in the liqueur.

FOR THE "BEANCURD"

225 g/8 oz whole almonds, blanched
2-3 oz/60-85 g sugar
   4 sheets gelatine
   • few drops almond essence
   • few drops almond oil

Grind the almonds to a paste and put them in a bowl. Pour 300 ml/10 fl oz boiling water over them and let it stand overnight. Next day, soften the gelatine in 140 ml/5 fl oz water. Put the sugar and a further 140 ml/5 fl oz water in a saucepan and stir until the sugar has dissolved. Stir in the softened gelatine and water and continue stirring until the gelatine has completely dissolved. Line a fine sieve with muslin or a jelly bag and pour in the almond mixture. Squeeze as much milky liquid out of the nuts as possible and mix it with the sweetened gelatine mixture. Add the almond essence.

Use almond oil to oil a clean shallow cake or baking tray and pour in the mixture. Chill in the refrigerator until set. Cut into lozenges or other shapes and serve in shallow glass bowls or plates, in a little syrup.

FIVE-SPICE
ALMOND CRISPS

Makes 24

110 g/4 oz ground almonds
15 g/½ oz rice flour
200 g/7 oz caster sugar
1 tsp five-spice powder
2 egg whites, lightly whisked

Line 2 baking sheets with rice paper. Mix together the dry ingredients and then fold in the egg whites until thoroughly blended. The mixture can be piped or spooned on to the baking trays. Leave plenty of room for the mixture to spread.

Bake at 180°C/350°F gas mark 4 for 20 minutes or until a pale golden brown. Cool on a wire rack.

These are delicious served with ice creams, sorbets, mousses and custards, and indeed on their own with a cup of tea or coffee.

LEMON GRASS
ALMOND CRISPS

You can make another version of this recipe by substituting finely ground dried lemon grass for five-spice powder.

LEMON GRASS AND
COCONUT CAKE

I rarely think of using herbs when making sweets and cakes, but a jar of dried lemon grass was next to the small bottle of sweet lemon oil when I went to get out my baking things one day. I had planned to make a lovely moist coconut cake, flavoured with lemon oil. A pinch of lemon grass made it even more fragrant. Serve it at teatime with a lemon water icing, or make a lemon syrup, pour it over the cake while still warm, cut into diamonds or triangles and serve it as a pudding.

Serves 8-10

170 g/6 oz unsalted butter, softened
170 g/6 oz light muscovado sugar
3 eggs, separated
85 g/3 oz self-raising flour ⎱
• pinch of salt   ⎰ sifted
1 tsp baking powder ⎰ together
110 g/4 oz desiccated coconut ⎰
1 tsp ground lemon juice
½ tsp lemon oil

Grease a 23 cm/9 inch square cake tin and line with greaseproof paper. Cream the butter and sugar together in a bowl and beat until pale and fluffy. Beat in the egg yolks, one at a time, then fold in the dry ingredients. Whisk the egg whites until stiff then fold into the cake mixture, together with the lemon oil. Pour into the prepared tin and bake in a preheated oven at 170°C/325°F gas mark 3 for 40-50 minutes or until a fine skewer inserted into the middle of the cake comes out clean. Allow the cake to cool slightly in the tin before removing it.

LEMON GRASS SOUFFLÉ

This is a baked soufflé allowed to go cold and served with a sauce. Prepare it the day before required or at least several hours in advance. The soufflé is also delicious served hot straight from the oven with a cold crème anglaise.

Serves 4-6

60 g/2 oz lemon grass
200 ml/7 fl oz water
170 g/6 oz unrefined granulated sugar
5 size 3 eggs
140 ml/5 fl oz full cream milk

Thinly slice the lemon grass and cook gently in the water until the fibres have become tender. Bring to the boil, remove from the heat and allow to steep for an hour. Put the mixture in a blender or food processor and process for 30 seconds. Strain into a saucepan. Stir in the sugar and heat gently until the sugar has melted and then cook to a thickish syrup, reducing by at least half. Cool.

Separate the eggs. Whisk the whites until stiff. Gradually sprinkle on half the syrup, gently folding it in with two forks. Pour the mixture into a large well buttered soufflé dish and bake in a preheated oven 190°C/375°F, gas mark 5 for 20-25 minutes.

Beat the egg yolks with the remaining syrup. Heat the milk to just boiling point and whisk into the egg mixture. Strain the mixture back into the saucepan and cool gently until slightly thickened but without letting it curdle. Remove the soufflé from the oven. Allow it to cool and then turn out on to a flat dish or dessert platter. Pour the sauce over it. Chill and serve.

SAGO PUDDING

The mixture of soft, bland sago, creamy coconut and a rich dark sugar syrup is quite irresistible. I always choose it in restaurants in Malaysia and Singapore and like to make it at home. The authentic gula melaka has a syrup made from the dark brown raw sugar or jaggery or the palmyra palm. At home I use a mixture of light and dark muscovado sugar or light muscovado and molasses sugar. The sago can be cooked in water, milk, skimmed milk or coconut juice or milk. In the Philippines, a much larger sago is used, the size of chickpeas, for a similar dish.

Serves 6

170 g/6 oz sago
430 ml/¾ pint milk or water
110 g/4 oz coconut cream
280 ml/½ pint full cream milk
170 g/6 oz dark sugars,
    as described above
170 ml/6 fl oz water
1 small piece fresh ginger
    or lemon grass

Cook the sago in the milk or water until soft. Pour into individual glass dishes and refrigerate until required. Heat the coconut cream and milk together. To make the syrup, whisk the sugar, water and ginger or lemon grass. Strain and allow to cool. To serve, pour the coconut cream around the edges of the sago puddings, make a well in the centre and pour in the syrup.

SUMMER FRUIT CONGÉE

This is an interpretation of a wonderful Chinese rice gruel or congée. Here the dish is made with tapioca and coconut milk and served chilled and lightly sweetened with jewel-like English summer berries suspended in it. It makes a marvellous ending to a summer lunch or dinner party. Make the coconut milk by pouring 570 ml/1 pint boiling water over the contents of a packet of desiccated coconut or the grated flesh from a fresh coconut, steeping it for 30 minutes and then forcing the liquid through a very fine sieve. Raspberries, red and white currants and alpine or wild strawberries are very good.

Serves 6-8

2 tbsp tapioca
570 ml/1 pint full cream milk or, even better, Channel Islands milk
1 bay leaf
1 vanilla pod
● sugar to taste
570 ml/1 pint coconut milk
455 g/1 lb berry fruit

Simmer the tapioca and milk with the bay leaf and vanilla pod until the tapioca is tender and translucent. This will take 30 minutes or so. Remove the bay leaf. Split the vanilla pod, and scrape the seeds into the tapioca. Sweeten the mixture to taste and stir in the coconut milk. The consistency should be quite soup-like. Thin down further with cream, if you wish. Stir in the fruit, which you will have first picked over and rinsed if necessary. Pour into a deep glass bowl and chill until required.

LIME CUSTARDS With MANGO SAUCE

Serves 4

2 fresh juicy limes
    with unblemished skins
85 g/3 oz silken tofu (beancurd)
2 size 2 eggs
● sugar or honey to taste
1 ripe mango

Peel off a few thin curls of lime zest and reserve for garnish. Grate the rest of the zest into the tofu. Beat in the two eggs. Squeeze the limes and beat the juice into the egg mixture. Sweeten the creamy mixture to taste. Pour into four small ramekins or dariole moulds (holding 75 ml/ 3 fl oz) which you have first brushed with a light neutral oil such as almond or grapeseed oil. Place in a steamer basket, cover and place over steam. Steam for about 8 minutes, depending on the depth of the containers.

Meanwhile, peel the mango, slice it, or spoon it into a blender and make a purée. The creams are done when a toothpick or knife point inserted into the centre comes out clean. You can serve them warm, cold or chilled, on a pool of mango sauce, decorated with blanched shreds of lime zest.

Overleaf: Lime Custards with Mango Sauce; Five-spice Almond Crisps (p. 159)

EIGHT TREASURE
RICE PUDDING

In the Orient, eight is a lucky number. My friend Karen Cox was married on 8.8.88, which was the most auspicious day possible in Hong Kong. This is a pudding for a special occasion with eight different treasures in it. You can only find seven fruits and nuts in the pudding? The eighth treasure is the rice, the most precious of all.

You can either cook it in a deep soufflé dish and serve it, like the more familiar rice pudding, with an appetizing brown skin on top, or you can par-cook the rice, pack it into a pudding basin with the other ingredients and steam it.

Serves 6-8

340 ml/12 fl oz skimmed milk
340 g/12 oz short-grain pudding rice
60-85 g/2-3 oz caster sugar
  60 g/2 oz clotted cream or
    extra thick cream
  60 g/2 oz crystallized
    ginger, chopped
  60 g/2 oz crystallized
    pineapple, chopped
  60 g/2 oz dried apricots or
    dried mango, chopped and soaked
    in hot water for 2-3 hours
  60 g/2 oz dates or dried figs, chopped
  60 g/2 oz blanched whole almonds, roughly
    chopped, or pine kernels
  60 g/2 oz unsalted pistachios or
    walnuts, roughly chopped
85 g/3 oz sweet bean paste

Put the milk and rice in a saucepan, bring to the boil and simmer for 15 minutes, by which time most of the milk will have been absorbed. If you are steaming the pudding, proceed as follows. Drain the rice and stir into it the sugar and cream. Mix in the rest of the ingredients and pack the mixture into a well-buttered pudding basin, about 750 ml/1½ pints. Tie on a piece of greaseproof paper or foil, pleated down the middle, and steam the pudding for about 1½ hours. Turn out on to a plate and serve with coconut cream, thin cream or almond syrup.

If you are cooking the pudding in the oven, do not drain the rice but stir in the sugar and cream together with the rest of the ingredients and cook for about 45 minutes at 180°C/350°F gas mark 4, covering the surface with a buttered paper or a piece of greaseproof paper if it shows signs of burning. In any case cook it towards the bottom of the oven.

EIGHT TREASURE WINTER
FRUIT CUSTARD

This is made in the same way as a traditional baked custard. It can be done either in a bain-marie in the oven or on top of the stove, or it can be steamed.

Serves 4-6

570 ml/1 pint milk
  1 cinnamon stick
  4 cloves
  4 allspice berries
  3 tbsp caster sugar
  4 eggs

THE "TREASURES"

*170 g/6 oz of the following, soaked
for 2 hours, dried, finely chopped
and mixed together*
- *stoned prunes, dates, figs, apricots,
peach, pear, apple*
- *plus 15 g/½ oz finely chopped
crystallized ginger*

Scald the milk with the cinnamon, cloves, allspice and caster sugar. Lightly beat the eggs and pour the scalding milk over them, beating all the time. Butter well 4 or 6 ramekins, divide the fruit among them and strain the custard over them. Cook very gently for 20-25 minutes or until a knife inserted in the centre comes out clean. Serve hot, warm or cold, as preferred. When cold, the custards can be turned out. An almond, ginger or jasmine syrup could be served with them.

ALMOND SYRUP

This can be served hot, warm or cold with puddings, cakes and fruit salads. It is particularly nice poured over freshly peeled lychees and left for an hour or so to chill, but it also goes well with the eight treasure rice pudding on p. 164.

Makes about 570 ml/1 pint

*15 g/½ oz cornflour
2 tbsp water
60 g/2 oz freshly ground almonds
570 ml/1 pint water
60 g/2 oz caster sugar*

Slake the cornflour with water and put it in a saucepan with the ground almonds and water. Stir to blend, then add the sugar. Bring to the boil, stirring, until the sugar has dissolved, and then simmer for 5 minutes. Leave to cool and chill until required. A more delicate syrup can be obtained by straining it through a muslin-lined sieve and squeezing out as much of the almond syrup as possible. It can also be flavoured with a little rosewater if liked.

JASMINE TEA SORBET

Use plenty of dried jasmine flowers, even if it means leaving the rest of the tea caddy rather bereft of flowers. You can use fresh white jasmine flowers.

Serves 4-6

*1 tbsp jasmine tea leaves and flowers
570 ml/1 pint water
225 g/8 oz golden granulated sugar
1 lemon, juice only*

Put the leaves and flowers in a bowl. Bring the water to the boil. Pour on and allow the tea to infuse for 8 minutes. Mix in the sugar and lemon juice and stir until the sugar has dissolved. Strain, cool and then freeze. This is delicious served with five-spice almond crisps, p. 159.

*Overleaf: Summer Fruit Congée (p. 161);
Eight Treasure Rice Pudding*

ACCOMPANIMENTS
TO
ORIENTAL FLAVOURS

WINES, SPIRITS AND OTHER DRINKS

There are probably more flavours in the western kitchen that are inimical to wine than in the oriental kitchen. Clearly, mouth-searing chillies are going to leave the palate in no state to be receptive to a crisp white Alsace or a fruity young Pomerol. But consider the difficulties of serving wines with egg-based dishes and with anything made with chocolate. Consider too the impossibility of matching wines to an artichoke-based dish. Salads and asparagus can also be problems.

Until very recently vineyards have not been part of China's agriculture and thus European-style wines have not traditionally accompanied meals. Teas, of a bewildering variety, are served before and after, and now, as a result of European customs, with the meal. Beer too is popular, as is fine cognac amongst the wealthy. Wines are now being made around Tsingtao (where some of the best beer of the same name is made) under that label and the Dynasty label. They are pleasant enough. Rice wines, particularly the fine Shaoxing, are good if potent companions to oriental food, especially, I think, in the winter. Nearer the equator I prefer to drink tea or the fine Tiger beer, Singha beer or Anchor beer.

However, fine oriental food deserves fine wines and I can think of no better illustration than to describe a meal cooked for us by our friend Carmel Chow in Hong Kong a few years ago:

1978 Auxey Duresses Les Boutonnières
Served with plain steamed prawns, which we dipped in a mixture
of soy sauce and chillies;

1979 Meursault
Served with steamed scallops and chopped fermented black beans,
spring onions and garlic;

1981 Chardonnay Reserve
Served with flowery crab, fried with ginger and spring onion;

1982 Chablis Grand Cru Blanchot
Served with the centrepiece, a baby grouper steamed with
coriander and spring onion with hot soy sauce and groundnut oil
sprinkled on top;
The same wine also accompanied Chinese mushrooms braised on a
bed of lettuce, with a little ginger and rice wine;

1983 Georges Duboeuf Pouilly Fuissé
Served with stir-fried Chinese spinach with garlic and a little chilli;

1976 Niersteiner Paterberg Beerenauslese
Served with the platter of tropical fruit.

Our experience since then has demonstrated that Chardonnay
wines are indeed among the best accompaniments to oriental
flavours. By extension, so is champagne of course. And so are the
good dry sparkling wines such as Prosecco from northeast Italy,
Blanquette de Limoux from southeast France and the Cava wines
from Penedes in northeast Spain.

Alsace and German wines have also been successful partners
with fish, chicken and pork dishes. And red wine is not to be ruled
out entirely. The braised lamb shanks on p. 122 for example, go
extremely well with a fruity young Bordeaux from Pomerol or St
Emilion, as do the quail dishes.

It surprises me that sherry is not more appreciated in the Far
East. As sherry vinegar makes a more than adequate substitute for
rice vinegar, so does sherry for rice wine, both in cooking and on
the table. A crisp fino or manzanilla is perfect with shellfish dishes
such as the cool and hot prawns (p. 80) and the scallop dishes (p.
89). Try a dry amontillado with the ginseng chicken on p. 101, and
a dry old oloroso with the roast Barbary duck on p. 116. A sweet
full oloroso or amoroso would go well with the eight treasure
custard on p. 164, as would a raisiny Pedro Ximenez.

Other flor influenced wines, such as those from the Jura, are fine companions to oriental food. And so is the legendary Château Grillet. A property of only 4 hectares, it produces very little wine, and is thus rarely found on wine lists. We have had the opportunity to try the magnificent 1975 vintage with exquisite dishes devised by Louis Outhier. He has worked and travelled in the Far East for many years, acting as consultant in a number of places, as he does in London at Ninety Park Lane. The brilliant manager of this restaurant, Sergio Rebecchi, selected the Château Grillet for us to drink with a cassolette of langoustines cooked with a coconut cream sauce flavoured with Thai herbs and spices, a dish which perfectly illustrates how to use oriental flavours in a western setting. The honeyed depth and fragrance of the wine, which continually reminds me of violets, fully stood up to the distinctive flavours and spicy sensations. It was memorable.

IMPLEMENTS

UTENSILS, GADGETS AND CONTAINERS

You do not need any special equipment for the recipes I have described. An ordinary domestic oven, gas or electric, or solid fuel; a gas or electric hob, the usual collection of knives, pots and pans and chopping boards, not to mention casseroles and serving dishes, will all be perfectly adequate. For as I have said elsewhere, this is not an oriental cookbook, it is a description of how to use oriental ingredients, flavours and ideas in your own kitchen.

However, if you are a keen cook, and an acquisitive, as well as an inquisitive cook, you will possibly already have a number of oriental utensils in your kitchen. Do you use them? Are they worth the cupboard space? A wok is a large implement, difficult to store, and does not really earn its keep if you use it only for the occasional stir-fry. I was ready to banish my wok to the attic when I discovered that it makes a brilliant jam pan, because it conducts heat well and has plenty of surface area for evaporation. I also use it for cooking homemade ravioli and gnocchi. In a deep conventional saucepan or stockpot I find they get crowded on top of each other, tending to stick together or break up. In a wok they have room to spread out and if you put the steamer rack on top, that keeps them submerged below the water. I have also cooked spaghetti and soup in the wok, as well as steaming chickens, custards and puddings in it. So yes, a wok is well worth having.

Two or three attractive bamboo steamer baskets that will fit inside your wok's domed lid mean that you can cook several dishes at once. On the other hand, these are not necessary if you already have a steamer set, either an electric one or one of those excellent stainless steel ones. An even simpler method of steaming is to use a large saucepan and put in it one of those folding steamer trays which open out like flower petals to fit the pan. Fish, vegetables, meat, custard pots, pudding basins, all can be satisfactorily steamed using this very simple equipment.

Steam boats and Mongolian hotpots, although attractive, will probably be about as much use as the '60s fondue set gathering dust in the bottom of a hard-to-get-at corner cupboard. For fondues and all those lovely, friendly "dip-dip" dishes, a sturdy enamel or cast iron casserole that will sit firmly on top of a table heater will do the job just as well. On the other hand, if you have been given a Mongolian hotpot, then perhaps it is time to make it a regular feature of your entertaining, perhaps for Sunday hotpot suppers.

Having learned from Chan Fat Chee how to use cleavers properly, I do enjoy the feel of them when I am chopping food, but I am not sure that they are any more efficient than my large cook's knife. And for certain tasks, such as making a stuffing for mushrooms or wonton, it has to be said that a food processor is perfectly adept at doing the job. Sharp knives, of the best quality that you can afford, are essential in any kitchen. Different shapes and sizes are needed for different tasks, not for a particular type of cuisine. A heavy handled and bladed chopping knife, a slender flexible filleting knife for fish, a stout, short-bladed boning knife for meat, a saw-edged knife for slicing and a small, sharp all-purpose knife should between them do most of the tasks. A vegetable peeler, a zester and a very fine serrated edged knife for peeling peaches and tomatoes are also useful.

Sieves and colanders are essential for straining sauces and draining noodles. A large spatula or shovel-shaped implement is useful for stir-frying and a mesh-headed implement something like a fishing net is useful for scooping out steamed or fried dumplings once they are cooked.

I have to admit to what I can only describe as an affectation when it comes to two particular utensils. I love using two-foot long chopsticks for cooking, all kinds of cooking. They are efficient, above all, but they also look quite elegant.

After one cocktail hour in Hong Kong, when we were sent canapés up to our room, I scoured the China Products Store in Queens Road, Central, for Chinese soup spoons of every colour and design. They are the perfect containers for cocktail snacks; a morsel of foie gras, a little ginger and crab, a scoop of caviar, a miniature steak tartare, a poached quail's egg on a potato cake. There is no need for forks, plates or napkins. Simply arrange the food on the spoons, and put the spoons on a plate or tray.

If you want to know what sort of table to lay for these dishes, western or oriental style, I would say it depends on your mood. I would not presume to prescribe what sort of tableware you should use. Sometimes I like to use large blue Japanese bowls, sometimes the white, petal-shaped bowls and chopsticks, more often our usual tableware which is not, and has never been a set, but just plates and bowls that go together. Large plates, shallow soup bowls and smaller plates should deal with just about every dish I have suggested. It will be obvious from the description of a dish whether to use plate service and which are best served family-style from a central dish or platter.

One item on my shopping list for the next trip to the Far East is bamboo soup cups. These are very eyecatching and perfect for cooking steamed soups and other dishes such as the minced quail on p. 112. An extra set could be used for steaming custards. But there, that's yet another shelf's worth of space taken up. And how often, to be honest, am I going to cook steamed soups and custards?

INDEX